Voices of the Race Riots: Beyond the Red Summer

TIFFANY B. LEE

Published by Black History Inc.

The way to right wrongs is to turn the light of the truth upon them. "-Ida B. Wells

Black Homes Decimated, Tulsa Race Riots
Photo Courtesy of Library of Congress

CONTENTS

People Searching for loved ones in a Mass Grave -- 1917 Race Riot

For three hundred years the Negroes of America have given their life blood to make the Republic the first among the nations of the world, and all along this time there has never been even one year of justice, but on the contrary a continuous round of oppression-

Marcus Garvey on the 1917 Race Riots

ACKNOWLEDGMENTS

I must acknowledge my mother, Roseland Marie Grimmett. She is the first person to encourage my writing. She was the person for me who Stephen King calls, "My Reader." I have since ventured away from the lighthearted stories that we talked about and have begun to cover Black History. One day, maybe I will return to those lighthearted stories; but currently, my heart is heavy.
I send love to my husband, Anwar and our son, Anwar.

CHAPTER 1:
DEDICATION TO THE VICTIMS OF RACE RIOTS

THIS IS DEDICATED TO OUR ANCESTORS, WHO WERE DENIED CITIZENSHIP, PERSONHOOD AND COMMON DIGNITY. THIS IS FOR THOSE WHO HELPED BUILD THIS COUNTRY BUT WERE DENIED BASIC HUMAN RIGHTS. ATTEMPTS AT BUILDING THEIR OWN COMMUNITIES WERE MET WITH INHUMANE BRUTALITY. LAWS WERE MADE TO DENY THEM PROPERTY OWNERSHIP, SUFFRAGE, AND EDUCATION; BUT THEY PERSEVERED.

HOWEVER, THIS PERSEVERANCE WAS MET WITH VICIOUS "BLACKLASH," WHICH IN MANY TOWNS ENDED WITH THE THREAT OF OR ACTUAL LYNCHING. IN OTHER TOWNS, A LYNCHING WAS ONLY THE BEGINNING. IT WAS A PRECURSOR FOR A RACE RIOT.

RACE RIOTS, RACE WARS, MASSACRES, OR ETHNIC CLEANSINGS WERE A BRUTAL FREE-FOR-ALL WHERE ANY PERSON: WOMAN, MAN OR CHILD COULD BE LYNCHED, STRANGLED, SHOT, OR BURNED TO DEATH BY A WHITE MOB, FOR SIMPLY WALKING DOWN THE STREET.

THEIR NEIGHBORS BEAR WITNESS TO THE DEPRAVITIES THEY SAW AND SUFFERED. THIS IS DEDICATED TO THE VICTIMS, MANY OF WHOM NEVER SAW THEIR ATTACKERS BE PUNISHED. THOUGH HARD TO READ AND HEAR, THESE WORDS MUST BE HEARD BY EVERYONE. THIS IS A TESTAMENT TO THE BRUTALITY AND CRUELTY THAT CAN HAPPEN WHEN HATE IS ALLOWED TO RULE. THIS IS WHAT CAN HAPPEN WHEN PEOPLE ARE SEEN AS "OTHER," AND THEREFORE, LESS THAN.

LET THEIR WORDS BE HEARD, LEST WE SEE A REOCCURRENCE. I DEDICATE THIS TO THE VICTIMS' LIVES…THEIR LEGACY.

A Copy of an intercepted *Letter* from Phillis to her Sister in the Country, describing the late Riot on Negro-Hill.

CHAPTER 2:
ORIGINS OF THE RACE RIOT
DEATH SENTENCE FOR IMMORALITY?

One of the earliest documented race riots occurred in Boston's West end neighborhood in 1815.[1] There is little information about this riot. The area of the riot was a working-class White and Black area referred to as "The Hill" or "Negro Hill." These lines from an 1816 Bobalition broadside, created to parody Black people as a whole and specifically the writer Phyllis Wheatley, offer some insight, "Dear Sisser, I hab sad tidings to enform you--O! a few night since I taught my lass day surely come--a great number de white truckerman got angre ... and threten to demolesh all de brack peeple housen!" (see picture at beginning of chapter and in the appendix). Greta LaFluer in *The Natural History of Sexuality in Early America* states that these riots in Boston were one of many "anti- brothel" riots that took place between the 1810s and the 1820s. Rioters and riot defenders claims of a populations' immortality is an excuse routinely given as justification for riots.

Immorality was used as the excuse for the 1824 riot which occurred in Providence, Rhode Island. Olney street included homes owned by Blacks and Whites. Many historical records identify the homes as brothels. Though Whites and Blacks visited the brothels, local politicians focused their ire on the Black population. The riot, which occurred on October 17, 1824, in an area commonly referred to as "Hard Scrabble."[2], started over the use of a sidewalk. The riot began because of the failure by Black's to move and allow a white person to walk on the sidewalk. A fight ensued between White and Black sailors with White sailors on the losing end.

In *The Life of William Brown,* he details an account as relayed to him by Augustus Williams:

> This story was told me by Augustus Williams, who was present and witnessed the whole affair and declared it to be the truth. The next visitation in Olney street was made by two crews of sailors, one white and the other colored, consequently a fight was the order of the day, in which the blacks were the conquerors, and drove the whites out of the street. The white sailors not relishing this kind of treatment, doubled their forces the next night and paid Olney street another visit, and had a general time of knocking down and dragging out. This mob conduct last-

ed for nearly a week. They greatly discomforted the saloon keepers, drinking their liquors, smashing up the decanters and other furniture. One of their number was shot dead by a bar tender, which so enraged them that they began to tear down houses, threatening to destroy every house occupied by colored people. Their destructive work extended through Olney street, Gaspee street and a place called the Hollow, neither of which bore a very good reputation. They warned the better class of colored people to move out and then went on with their work of destruction, calling on men of like principles, from other towns, to

help, promising to share with them in the plunder, or take their pay from the banks. Governor Arnold hearing of this ordered out the military, thinking that their presence would quell the mob. They were not so easily frightened, and continued their work of ruin until the governor was compelled to order his men to fire. This had the desired effect; broke up the riot and dispersed the mob; but Olney street had fallen to rise no more as a place of resort for rum shops, sailors and lewd women.

BROWN FURTHER REFERS TO THIS AS THE RIOT WHICH WOULD BRING AN END TO THE STREET'S EXISTENCE ENTIRELY.

According to ric.edu, the "Town Watch" refused to intervene and keep the peace, which may be the reason the Governor called for troops to intervene as noted in this account. This failure to intervene left citizens unprotected during the riot, and rioters faced minimal repercussions. Some rioters refused to be tried for what they believed were not crimes, and simply did not go to court.. The rioters Defense Attorney, Joseph L. Tillinghast argued that the mob was serving the public by restoring proper moral character. Of the fifty or more rioters, most received no punishment for their crimes.

The 1824 Riot Mirrored Other Riots in Several Ways:

Prior to the riots:
- False accusations of Blacks being immoral or violent
- Blacks in the area attempting to assert their rights.
- Previous violence towards Blacks in the area.
- Failure by law enforcement or political figures to punish those accused of assaults against Blacks, establishing a pattern that violence against Black citizens would be tolerated

During the Riots:
- Killing of Black citizens
- Destruction of Black citizens' property.
- Failure by law enforcement and local government to protect Black citizens or their property
- Justification of the rioters' inhumane behavior as working on behalf of the community against a perceived threat.

After the Riots:
- Failure to adequately prosecute white rioters. According to *Sundown Towns: A Hidden Dimension of American Racism*[3], this would embolden rioters and lead to repeated riots in the same town or nearby town.
- Repeated victimization of the same Black population, either in the same town or in another town.

Documented incidents in Providence, Rhode Island <u>Prior to the 1824 Race Riot:</u>

On page 86 of *The Life of William Brown*, he states that Black citizens built a school for their children, then began to purchase property. Whites believed that since Blacks were acquiring property, they should pay tax. The Black population said, "No taxation without representation." It was believed that Black people should not have the same rights as Whites and any suggestion of rights for Blacks was looked upon unfavorably. Whites refused to allow a "Nigger's" vote to count the same as theirs. His account is noted:

After the feeling was understood by those who had spoken, they appointed a committee to meet the next general assembly, and inform them of their disapproval to meet the tax, for they believed taxation and representation went together; and they were unwilling to be taxed and not allowed to be represented. Some of the members of the house said it was perfectly right; if the colored people were to be taxed they should be represented. But the members of the house from Newport were bitterly opposed to colored people being represented, saying: "Shall a Nigger be allowed to go to the polls and tie my vote? No, Mr. Speaker, it can't be. The taxes don't amount to more than forty or fifty dollars; let them be taken off." So the taxes were taken off.

At that time the colored people had little or no protection. It was thought a disgrace to plead a colored man's cause, or aid in getting his rights as a citizen, or to teach their children in schools. The teachers themselves were ashamed to have it known that they taught colored schools.

The riots in Boston and Rhode Island are some of the earliest documented but are not the first. There are many reasons why race riots have gone undocumented. As noted in the book *Sundown Towns,* prior to most towns becoming 'Sundown Towns', there is a large dip in the Black population which could only have been precipitated by an event of some kind; however, the town has suppressed this history. Another reason they have gone undocumented is that there was no official name for these attacks. Some are referred to as race riots, others are referred to as 'mob attacks' and others may not be noted as they were unfortunately and accepted practice used to rid the city of its unwanted Black population. For these reasons, it may be hard to understand when and where race riots actually took place. In *The Life of William Brown*, he notes other incidences of violence against the Black population which should also be referred to as Race Riots, but the confrontation is instead referred to as a mob attack.

He speaks of one victim in particular, Christopher Hall:

> At last disturbances became so common that they raised a mob, and drove many from their houses, then tore them down, took their furniture— what little they had—carried it to Pawtucket, and sold it at auction. This was done late in the fall. One colored man named Christopher Hall, a widower with three or four children, a pious man, bearing a good character, and supported himself and family by sawing wood, had his house torn down by the roughs and stripped of its contents. He drew the roof over the cellar, and lived in it all winter. The people

tried in vain to coax him out, and offered him a house to live in. Many went up to see the ruins, among them some white ladies, who offered to take his children and bring them up, but he would not let them go. In the spring following he went to Liberia, on the western coast of Africa. Not long after this there was another mob, commenced at the west end of Olney street.

According to these records, Brown speaks of two mob attacks happening prior to the riot of 1824. which Brown states is the one that resulted in the end of Olney Street. The reason why Brown considered two as 'mob attacks' and one as a riot is unknown. Possibly the scope of destruction and amount of lives lost would account for the difference in what was considered as a riot versus a mob attack. It is clear though that Brown does not consider the two differently: The violence, and property destruction are described similarly; however, researchers and city historians note only an 1824 and 1831 riot. There are no previous riots listed.

As stated in the *Encyclopedia of Race Riots*[4], the 1831 Race Riot was instigated by white sailors that "obliterated a black community"(45). Providence, Rhode Island sadly is one of many cities where the Black population was decimated more than once in less than a decade.

CHAPTER 3:

CINCINNATI: REPEATED DEVASTATION
DESTRUCTION OF THE FIRST BLACK WALL STREET?

JOHN MERCER LANGSTON

Cincinnati, Ohio is historically known to have had one of the largest free Black populations prior to the Emancipation. The community served as a conduit on the Underground Railroad and was the home to many successful Black people who would bond together to purchase property, businesses and pay for enslaved relatives to be released from bondage. John Mercer Langston in his book, *From the Virginia Plantation to the National Capital* says,

> "If there has ever existed in any colored community of the United States, anything like an aristocratic class of such persons, it was found in Cincinnati at the time to which reference is here made [the 1830's]. Besides finding there then a large class of such persons, composed in greater part of good-looking, well dressed and well-behaved young people of considerable accomplishment, one could count many families possessing a reasonable amount of means, who bore themselves seemingly in consciousness of their personal dignity and social worth" (61-62).

Langston, himself a member of this wealthy class, who was young during the riot described in his account would go on to become a civil rights leader, President of Howard University School of Law, and a congressman. The growing successful Black population in Cincinnati was seen as a threat to local Whites which made them a target and victims of race riots in 1829, 1836, 1841, and 1862.

The late twenties through the '40s proved to be a tumultuous time. White mobs attacked not only Blacks, but Black sympathizers. Paul Gilje, in *Rioting in America[5]* states, "During a pogrom in Cincinnati, August 16-22, 1829, in which one white was killed, the invasion of the African-American district forced hundreds of blacks from their homes" (89). Langston and other sources state that in 1841, a white mob, threw the press of Dr. Gamaliel Bailey's, abolitionist paper *The Philanthropist* into the Ohio River.

Black success continued to draw the ire of their white counterparts, Irish immigrants who were newly immigrating to the country ravished the Black Community. There were at least two entrepreneurs, William Watson and Henry Boyd whose financial status would place them as that of millionaires today, according to *Race and the City: Work, Community, and Protest in Cincinnati, 1820-1970[6]*. Boyd's furniture factory was burned so many times that in 1859, he had to shutter his furniture business because no insurer would provide him with insurance. However, the community flourished despite the backlash. The Black population continued to acquire property individually and through a joint stock enterprise named the Iron Chest Company, which purchased property and rented to whites. Blacks in the community banded together not only economically but began social programs to uplift other Blacks in the community. Those of means provided education to those in need in the community and worked on a national level to abolish slavery. One person who was offered education stated, "Before I commenced schools, I did not feel any interest in laying up property. I did not feel that I had a home here. If I earned property, I knew not but my house would be pulled down over my head by a mob" (as qtd. in *Race and the City*).

What follows are accounts of the 1841 Race Riot. *Race and the City* states this riot may have been one of the most devastating pre-civil war riots in history. The Black community was devastated financially, with *Race and the City* noting an over 50,000 dollar drop in the real estate holdings of the Black community. Many city leaders left for Canada and formed the small settlement in Canada, later named Wilberforce. Those who stayed were no longer as outspoken about abolition for fear of jeopardizing their lives and livelihood. Sadly, the community that escaped to Wilberforce were also the victims of Irish mobs in Canada.

John Mercer Langston refers to this chapter as "The Great Change" for the devastation that the riots caused to the community. It should be noted that his date of 1840 is off by one year, as several resources documented the riot occurring in 1841. His recollection of the exact year may be related to his younger age at the time of the incident, and older age at the time of writing the book.

THE GREAT CHANGE! 63

and sustain such mob-spirit as ultimately showed itself in murderous, destructive methods.

The last outbreak of this character, which John was permitted to witness and which made a lasting impression upon his youthful mind, was that in which the press of Dr. Gamaliel Bailey, the editor and publisher of the "Philanthropist," was seized and by the infuriated rabble thrown into the Ohio river. For several weeks feeling against the Abolitionists, so-called, friends of the colored people, and against the colored people themselves, had been showing itself in high and open threats, conveyed in vulgar, base expressions, which indicated the possibility and probability of an early attack upon both the classes mentioned.

It was early upon a certain Friday evening, in the late fall of 1840, that excited groups of men, some white and others colored, were seen about the streets of the city and showing by their words and gesticulations, that their minds were dwelling upon, and that they were stirred by some deeply serious and fearful matter. By reason of the fact that many found among the white classes were strangers, and evidently persons from the State of Kentucky; and the further fact that the colored people seemed to be specially moved by the apprehensions of assault, which they feared might be coming upon them and their friends, one could very easily understand that the mob, which had been expected, was about to show itself. Such fear proved to be well grounded; for about nine o'clock, a large ruffianly company, coming over from the adjacent towns of Kentucky, called together a large number of the baser sort of the people of Cincinnati, and opened, without the least delay, an outrageous, barbarous and deadly attack upon the entire class of the colored people. They were assaulted wherever found upon the streets, and with such weapons and violence as to cause death in many cases, no respect being had to the character, position, or innocence of those attacked. The only circumstance that seemed necessary to provoke assault, resulting even in death, was the color of the person thus treated.

After the first sudden surprising attack, the colored people, measurably prepared for such occurrence by reason of the condition of public feeling manifested latterly, as already described, certainly in their expectations of it, aroused themselves, seized any means of defence within their reach, and with manliness and courage met their assailants. One of their number, Major Wilkerson, was made their leader; and never did man exhibit on the field of danger greater coolness, skill and bravery, than this champion of his people's cause. A negro himself, he fought in self-defence, and to maintain his own rights as well as those of the people whom he led. They had full confidence in his ability, sincerity, courage and devotion, and were ready to follow him even to death. The record of the number of deaths which occurred during that eventful night, among both the white and the colored people, can never be made. It is well known, however, that the desperate fighting qualities of the latter class were fully demonstrated in the great number of fatal casualties which were noted. All night the fight continued. Many of the white attacking party were carried directly from the fight to the grave; and not a few of the colored men fell in gallant manner, in the struggle which they made in their own defence.

Saturday morning as it dawned upon the stricken city, witnessed a lull in the struggle; and many felt and hoped that the riot with its frightful incidents had ceased. But the day had not grown old before by regulation of the city authorities, swarms of improvised police-officers appeared in every quarter, armed with power and commission to arrest every colored man who could be found. It was claimed that these arrests were made for the purpose of protecting such persons against the further attacks of the mob. Such, however, was by no means the case. The arrests were made, and the colored men were imprisoned, because it had been thoroughly shown by their conduct that they had become so determined to protect themselves against whatever odds, that great and serious damage might be expected were they again assaulted. Hundreds of them concealed themselves at home, and in other hiding-places, and thus escaped arrest.

Early in the day, the family of Mr. John Woodson, living across the canal in Broadway, in that part of the city known as "Germany," and where John boarded at the time, was visited by a colored neighbor, who called to tell Mr. Woodson what was occurring as to the arrest of the colored men, and to advise him both to conceal himself, and to have his foreman, Mr. John Tinsley, do the same thing. The boy waited to see Mr. Woodson hide himself in one chimney of his house, and Mr. Tinsley in another, when he told them both good-bye; and leaving the house through the back yard and garden, jumped over the fence into the alley, and made his way as rapidly as possible, by Main Street, to the canal bridge. He had reached the middle of the bridge crossing the canal, when he heard behind him the voice of officers ordering him to stop. Fleet of foot, with his speed quickened by such orders, he ran with all his might, without the least abatement of his speed, over a mile, to the corner of Main and Fourth Streets, where he entered a drugstore, through which he was compelled to pass to reach his brother Gideon. His brother was concealed at the time, with five other colored men, employed by him in a barber-shop, which he owned and conducted, located near this point. Overcome by excitement and fatigue, no longer in control of his powers, the boy fell to the floor of the drugstore, as if dead, alarming those in charge there, who, seeing his condition, came at once to his relief. He was carried thence into the rooms of his brother, just at hand, where he was cared for, with restoratives promptly administered, and soon recovered himself.

His brother's shop was closed and fortified to the extent of his ability, as to doors and windows, when it ought to have been opened and all the men at work. All found there were agitated, disturbed and anxious about their safety. The arrival of the boy, with such experience as he had to describe after his recovery, did little, indeed, toward reassuring these frightened persons. They feared that the boy would be pursued and they be found and arrested. Subsequent events showed, however, that the good men who kept the drugstore mentioned, were watchful of their interests and ready to protect them against harm. As the night came on, and the darkness rendered it practicable to do so, the owners of the store took John out with them to a confectionery, not far distant, where they purchased a full supply of needed edibles, which, under their care and protection, he carried to his brother and his men, then hungry enough from fasting for more than fifteen hours.

The diabolism of this mob reached its highest pitch, when thousands of infuriated, ungovernable ruffians, made mad by their hatred of the negro and his friends, came down Main Street with howls, and yells, and screams, and oaths, and vulgarities, dragging the press of Dr. Bailey, the great Abolition editor, which they threw, in malignant, Satanic triumph, into the river.

The days and nights made memorable by the deeds here detailed, must ever stand as the blackest and most detestable in the history of the great city of Cincinnati! And how all the black features which distinguish and intensify their horrid character, forever stand impressed upon the memory of the lad who witnessed, as he was terrified by them!

Such cowardly and unjustifiable abuse of their white friends and attack on the colored men, did not tend in the slightest degree to destroy the growing anti-slavery sentiment of Cincinnati and Ohio. Lewis, Chase, Hayes, Smith and other great leaders of the Abolition movement were made thereby the bolder, braver, more outspoken and eloquent in their utterances in such behalf. Nor did such treatment close the lips and hush the voices of the eloquent colored men themselves, who through such experiences, were learning what their rights were, and how to advocate and defend them. It was about this time that the black orator, John I Gaines, made his debut upon the platform, pleading the cause of his people; that Joseph Henry Perkins, another

colored speaker of fine talent and great eloquence, appeared
in his early efforts of the same character; that Andrew J.
Gordon, of the same class, not only discovered signal ability
with his pen, but unusual power with his tongue, as the
negro's defender; and that Gideon Q. Langston, also
manifested large ability and learning with commanding and
surprising qualities of oratory, in advocating the cause of
his race. Other names of this class might be mentioned
here, as fearless and able defenders of the rights of their
people, all of whom, it was the privilege and advantage of
the boy John to hear and know, their eloquent efforts serving him in large measure as inspiration and purpose.

The Sabbath following these occurrences was one of the
greatest beauty and loveliness. The quiet of the city was
truly impressive; and but for the hundreds of horsemen,
the mounted constabulary forces found necessary to parade
the streets and maintain the good order of the city, while
protecting the lives of its people, it would have been a day
fit for the calm and peaceful worship of our Heavenly
Father in a civilized and Christian community. As it was,
however, the horrid sight of the vast company of such
policemen, the solemn, awful tread and tramp of their
march, with the recollection of the sad, dire events of the
preceding nights and days, drove every feeling of love and
veneration out of the hearts of those who had thus been
outraged and terrified.

Those were dark days! And they who still survive them,
may never forget the circumstances of their occurrence, and
the public sentiment, which, no longer prevalent, made them
possible at that time!

Newspaper Account:

1841:
[Cincinnati Daily Gazette, September 6, 1841]

RIOT AND MOBS, CONFUSION AND BLOOD SHED

This city has been in a most alarming condition for several days—and from about 8 o'clock on Friday evening until about 3 o'clock yesterday morning, almost entirely at the mercy of a lawless mob ranging in number, from two to fifteen hundred. Amidst the confusion of such a state of things, it is almost impossible to collect a full or accurate state of facts. But with deep regret, and acknowledged humiliation, we detail what has happened as well as we can.

On Tuesday evening last, as we are informed, a quarrel took place near the corner of Sixth street and Broadway, between a party of Irishmen, and some negroes in which blows were exchanged, and other weapons, if not fire arms, used. Some two or three of each party were wounded. On Wednesday night the quarrel was renewed in some way, and sometime after midnight, a party of excited men armed with clubs attacked a house occupied as a negro boarding house on MacAlister street, demanding the surrender of a negro, whom they said had fled into the house, and was there secreted, and uttering the most violent threats against the house, and the negroes in general. Several of the adjoining houses were occupied by negro families, including a number of women and children. The violence increased and was resisted by those in or about the houses—an engagement took place several were wounded on each side—and some say guns or pistols were discharged from the house. The interference of some gentlemen in the neighborhood succeeded in restoring quiet after about three fourths of an hour, when a watchman appeared. But it is singular, that this violent street disturbance elicited no report to the police nor arrest—indeed that the Mayor remained ignorant of the affair, until late in the day, when he casually heard of it.

On Thursday night another recontre took place in the neighborhood of the Lower Market, between some young men and boys, and some negroes, in which one or two of the boys were badly wounded, as was supposed, with knives—how the negroes fared, we did not learn.

On Friday during the day, there was considerable excitement. Threats of violence and lawless outbreak were indicated in various ways, and came to the ear of the police and of the negroes. Attacks were expected upon the negro residences in MacAlaster, Sixth and New streets. The negroes armed themselves and the knowledge of this increased the excitement. But we do not know that it produced any known measure of precaution on the part of the police, to preserve the peace of the city.

Before eight o'clock in the evening, a mob, the principal organization of which, we understand was arranged in Kentucky, openly assembled in Fifth Street Market, unmolested by the police or citizens. The number of this mob, as they deliberately marched from their rendezvous towards Broadway and Sixth streets, is variously estimated, but the number increased as they progressed. They were armed with clubs and stones.

Reaching the scene of operations with shouts and blasphemous imprecations, they attacked a negro confectionary house on Broadway, next to Sycamore, and demolished the doors and windows. This attracted an immense crowd. Savage yells were uttered to encourage the mob onward to the general attack upon the negroes. About this time, before 8 o'clock, J.W. Piatt, in a way, highly creditable to himself addressed the mob exhorting them to peace, obedience to law, and to retire without further violence. His voice was drowned by the violent shouts of the mob, and the throwing of stones…The Mayor came up and addressed the people, in a very proper way. The savage yell was instantly raised—"down with him!"—"run him off"—were shouted and intermixed with horrid imprecations and exhortations to the mob to move onward. We took some pains to ascertain who these leading disturbers of the peace were, and think a large portion of the leaders, and the most violent, came from the other parts were strangers—some were said to be connected with river navigation and were strongly backed by boat hands of the lowest and most violent order. They advanced to the attack with stones and were repeatedly fired upon by the negroes. The mob scattered, but immediately rallied again, and again were in like manner repulsed. Men were wounded on both sides, and carried off—and many reported dead. The negroes rallied several times, advanced upon the crowd, and most unjustifiably fired down the street into it, causing a great rush down the street. These things were repeated until past 1 o'clock, when a party procured an iron six pounder from near the river, loaded with boiler punchings, and hauled it to the ground, against the exhortations of the Mayor and others. It was posted on Broadway and pointed down Sixth street.
The yells continued, but there was a partial cessation of the firing. Many of the negroes had fled to the hills. The attack upon houses was recommenced, with the firing of guns, on both sides, which continued during most of the night—and exaggerated rumors of the killed and wounded filled the streets. The cannon was discharged several times.

About two o'clock, a portion of the military upon the call of the Mayor proceeded to the scene of disorder and succeeded in keeping the mob at bay…

A meeting of citizens was held at the Court House on Saturday morning, at which the Mayor presided. This meeting was addressed by the Mayor, Judge Read, Mr. Piatt, Sheriff Avery, and Mr. Hart. They resolved to observe the law, to discountenance mobs, invoked the aid of the civil authorities to stay the violence, and pledged themselves to exertion in aid of the civil authority to arrest and place within reach of the law, the negroes who wounded the two white boys on Columbia street…

The City Council also held a special session, and passed resolutions invoking the united exertions of orderly citizens to the aid of the authorities—to put down the violent commotion existing in the city, to preserve order and vindicate the law against the violence of an excited and lawless mob—requesting all officers, watchmen, and firemen to unite for the arrest of all rioters and violators of law, and the Marshal to increase his deputies to any number required, not exceeding five hundred, to preserve life and protect property—requiring the Mayor and Marshal to call in the aid of the county militia to preserve order, and the Captain of the Watch to increase his force…

The negroes held a meeting in a church and respectfully assured the Mayor and the citizens that they would use every effort to conduct as orderly, industrious, and peaceable people, and to suppress any imprudent conduct among their population and to ferret out all violation of order and law—deprecated the practice of carrying about their person any dangerous weapon, pledged themselves not to carry or keep any about their persons or houses and expressed their readiness to surrender all such...

Some then supposed we should have a quiet night—but others more observing, discovered that the lawless mob had determined on further violence, to be enacted immediately after nightfall. Citizens disposed to aid the authorities were invited to assemble, enroll themselves, and organize for action. The Military were ordered out, firemen were out clothed with authority as a police band. About 80 citizens enrolled themselves as assistants of the Marshal, and acted during the night under his directions, in connection with Judge Torrence, who was selected by themselves. A portion of this force was mounted. A troop of horse, and several companies of volunteer infantry continued on duty until near midnight...

As was anticipated, the mob efficiently organized early, commenced operations, dividing their force and making attacks at different points, thus distracting the attention of the police. The first successful onset was made upon the printing establishment of the Philanthropist. They succeeded in entering the establishment breaking up the Press, and running with it, amidst savage yells, down through Main street to the river, into which it was thrown. The military appeared in the alley near the office, interrupting the mob for a short time. They escaped through the by ways and, when the military retired, returned to their work of destruction in the office, which they completed. Several houses were broken open in different parts of the city, occupied by negroes, and the windows, doors and furniture totally destroyed.

Among such is the Confectionary establishment, of Burnet near the upper market—a shop on Columbia near Sycamore—the negro church on 6th street, and four or five houses near it—a small frame house near the synagogue on Broadway, and several houses on Western Row near the river. One of their last efforts was to fire or otherwise destroy the Book establishment of Messrs. Truman and Smith, on Main. From this they were driven by the police, and soon after, before daylight, dispersed from mere exhaustion, whether to remain quiet or to recruit their strength for renewed assault we may know before this paper is circulated.

Mortifying as is the declaration, truth requires us to acknowledge, that our good city has been in complete anarchy, controlled mostly by a lawless and violent mob for twenty-four hours, trampling all law and authority underfoot. We feel this degradation deeply—but so it is. It is impossible to learn the precise number killed and wounded, either of whites or among the negroes, probably several were killed on both sides, and some twenty or thirty variously wounded, though but few dangerously. Several of the citizen police were hurt with stones and brick bats, which were thrown into the crowd by the mob. The authorities succeeded in arresting and securing about forty of the mob, who are now in prison—others were arrested, but were rescued or made their escape otherwise. We have attempted a plain general narrative of these disgraceful proceedings—have endeavored to be accurate in our facts, and to narrate them in the order of occurrence without coloring or distortion. Such a narrative, at this time, we thought necessary to check the exaggerated rumors which have doubtless spread in all directions. Many of these transactions occurred under our own observation, during Friday night, and the evening and night of Saturday.

We see in these outrages much to deplore, and we see much which merits unqualified condemnation, which has been done, and omitted, during the violence of these lawless excesses. But it behooves us all now to be calm, and firm, to prevent another outbreak—to unite and draw out for the preservation of the public peace, all good citizens. Many have hitherto done little to stop destructive violence, who should unite, and we still trust nearly all will yet unite, to restore the quiet of the city, and the efficacy of the law….

CHAPTER 4:
THE DRAFT RIOTS
WERE RACE RELATIONS IN THE NORTH BETTER THAN THE SOUTH?

During the Civil War, many Americans elected to join the Union Army. So many, in fact, that the Army halted enlistments; however, as the war raged on, economic loss and loss of life grew exponentially causing the war to become highly unpopular amongst American citizens. Therefore, when the Union needed more soldiers, there were few willing to enlist. This forced the government to begin the draft. As expected, the draft was detested by the general public and led to riots throughout the country. Some riots, like the one in Ozaukee County, Wisconsin were targeted towards White Governmental officials. Though there was significant damage to property, there was no loss of life, the military was quickly involved (within a matter of hours), and all rioters were immediately imprisoned. This is significantly different than draft riots that targeted Black citizens.

Other draft riots were not directed towards the government but were instead directed towards Blacks within the town. Two draft riots in 1863 are of great significance, the Detroit Draft Riots and the New York City Draft Riots. In Detroit, it is believed that the *Detroit Free Press* newspaper was part to blame for the riots as they stated that recently freed Blacks, whom the writers regularly referred to as NIGGERS, were violent and unruly. The case of William Faulkner would prove to be the final excuse for the mob to attack.[7] Faulkner was accused of assaulting two young girls, one White and one Black. The mob gathered around the courthouse. While Faulkner was being transported, one of the guards shot a member of the mob, which resulted in the mob attacking the Black neighborhood. According to the *Nottinghamshire Guardian*, "Many unoffending coloured men were murdered. 32 negro houses were burnt or otherwise destroyed, and 200 people rendered homeless."[8]

The New York City Draft Riots lasted from July 13th to July 17th of 1863. According to *The Encyclopedia of Race Riots*, most of the rioters were white protestants and Irish Catholic immigrants who were against the war and did not want slavery to end. Rioters attacked and lynched Blacks indiscriminately, drove thousands of Blacks from the city and savagely attacked a Black Orphanage. *The Encyclopedia of Race Riots*[9] refers to this as a pogrom, and defines pogrom as,"...a unilateral relentless attack to obliterate the black community"(xxiii). It is further stated in this source that pogroms occurred because Blacks challenged the "color line in politics, economics or status." Over 120 Blacks were killed during the riots.

During the New York City Riot, John Perry was a Union Surgeon who was recovering from a broken leg. He and his wife Martha were unaware of the tension that had been building in the city. Both Martha and her husband are white. John was heavily sedated and unaware of the danger early on. The information that appears are Martha's words of her experience during the riots.

The following is an account from *Letters of a Surgeon.*

OF THE CIVIL WAR

CHAPTER IV

THE NEW YORK RIOT

(Described by Mrs. Perry)

AFTER this experience my husband was laid up at home for several weeks, waiting with keen impatience for the time when he could return to his regiment. This quiet period of inaction was, however, broken by the New York Riot, which took place in the month of July, 1863. The disturbance was due to the draft made necessary by the dearth of volunteers, and also to the fear among the Irish that the negroes at the South would come North and crowd them out of their work. While it lasted the foreign, and especially the Irish, element of the city had complete control. For more than a week lawlessness reigned supreme, and though

57

LETTERS FROM A SURGEON

our experience was far less severe than that of many others, those who were not born when these events took place may be interested to read quotations from a letter written by me to relatives in Boston.

NEW YORK, July 20th, 1863.

Strange to say, although we knew of the intense excitement in the city and heard that many of our neighbors had been up every night, too terrified to rest, we had no idea of personal danger.

On the first day of the riot, in the early morning, I heard loud and continued cheers at the head of the street, and supposed it must be news of some great victory. In considerable excitement I hurried downstairs to hear particulars, but soon found that the shouts came from the rioters who were on their way to work. About noon that same day we became aware of a confused roar; as it increased, I flew to the window, and saw rushing up Lexington

58

OF THE CIVIL WAR

Avenue, within a few paces of our house, a great mob of men, women, and children; the men, in red working shirts, looking fairly fiendish as they brandished clubs, threw stones, and fired pistols. Many of the women had babies in their arms, and all of them were completely lawless as they swept on.

I drew the cot upon which John was lying, his injured leg in a plaster cast, up to the window, and threw his military coat over his shoulders, utterly unconscious of the fact that if the shoulder straps had been noticed by the rioters they would have shot him, so blind was their fury against the army. The mass of humanity soon passed, setting fire to several houses quite near us, for no other reason, we heard afterward, than that a policeman, whom they suddenly saw and chased, ran inside one of the gates, hoping to find refuge. The poor man was almost beaten to death, and the house, with those adjoining, burned.

59

LETTERS FROM A SURGEON

At all points fires burst forth, and that night the city was illuminated by them. I counted from the roof of our house five fires just about us, but our own danger in all this tumult, strangely enough, never crossed our minds.

The next day was a fearful one. Men, both colored and white, were murdered within two blocks of us, some being hung to the nearest lamp-post, and others shot. An army officer was walking in the street near our house, when a rioter was seen to kneel on the sidewalk, take aim, fire, and kill him, then coolly start on his way unmolested. I saw the Third Avenue street car rails torn up by the mob. Throughout the day there were frequent conflicts between the military and the rioters, in which the latter were often victorious, being partially organized, and well armed with various weapons taken from the stores they had plundered.

I passed the hours of that dreadful night

60

OF THE CIVIL WAR

listening to the bedlam about us; to the drunken yells and coarse laughter of rioters wandering aimlessly through the streets, and to the shouts of a mob plundering houses a block away, from which, as we heard later, the owners barely escaped with their lives. I must confess that as I lay in the darkness amid the uproar, there was some feeling of shelter, yes, and even rest, in having the sheet well drawn over my head, and this with no sense of heat or suffocation, although the mercury stood very high.

The next morning's news was that the rioters were murdering the colored people wherever found, and that there was no limit to the atrocities committed against them. Hurrying to the kitchen, I found our colored servants ghastly with terror, and cautioned them to keep closely within doors. One of them told me that she had ventured out early that morning to clean the front door, and that the passing

61

LETTERS FROM A SURGEON

Irish, both men and women, had sworn at her so violently, saying that she and her like had caused all the trouble, that she finally rushed into the house for shelter.

Now that I began to realize our danger, I tried with all my power to keep John in ignorance of it, for in his absolutely disabled condition the situation was most distressing. The heat was intense; and during the morning I sat in his room behind closed window-shutters, continually on the alert to catch every outside noise, while watching the hot street below in the glare of sunlight. On the steps of an opposite house I recognized a policeman, whose usual beat was through our street, sitting in his shirt sleeves without any sign of uniform, looking rough and disorderly, and talking to the strolling bands of rioters. I wondered whether he was doing detective service, or whether he had joined the lawless mob. Men and women passed

62

9999

LETTERS FROM A SURGEON

my life without a moment's conscious gratitude. If our lives were now spared should I ever again be so unmindful?

When one of my brothers returned to lunch and reported the increasing strength of the mob, I told him of all I had seen and heard during the morning, and we considered the question of barricading the street doors and windows, but soon decided that it was useless. He then went to the police station to ask for information and help, but before leaving placed a ladder against the wall of our back yard, so that in case of attack the servants might, by this means, escape to the adjoining premises, and from there to the next street. At the police station my brother was told that, through one of their detectives who had been working in our street all the morning, they had learned that their station and also our house, with the one opposite, were to be attacked and burned that night, all being in close proximity.

64

OF THE CIVIL WAR

The police had been already plundered of most of their firearms, and needed all their force to defend themselves. They could do literally nothing for us, but recommended barricading the front entrances to the house as well as we could.

The afternoon wore on, and, feeling somewhat restless from the helpless inactivity at such a time, I wandered into the different rooms of the house, looked at our valuables, locked some in trunks, tucked a few trinkets and a roll of bills into my gown, and then returned to the window-seat, feeling a little weighted with value, but better satisfied.

The city became frightfully still, and this silence was broken only by occasional screams and sharp reports of musketry.

By this time John knew pretty clearly the condition of things. He had heard the shouts in the street, and in spite of my efforts surmised the rest. The stillness grew so intense that the very atmos-

5   65

LETTERS FROM A SURGEON

phere seemed a part of it, for not a breath of air stirred. As our landlord lived in the same block with us, it occurred to my brothers that in case of an attack we might escape over the roofs and pass down the skylight of his house, knowing that the very urgency of the situation would enable us to carry John with us somehow; but this privilege was refused, as the man said it might endanger his family.

My brothers were calling at every house in the ward to induce the occupants to meet at the police station, armed with whatever weapon each could find, in order to organize and patrol the streets through the night. Meantime, our servants were instructed to remain downstairs, and not to run until the house was actually attacked, then to rush for the ladder in the back yard; and I was to cover their retreat by hiding the ladder.

These plans and directions seemed to me at the time perfectly reasonable and pos-

66

OF THE CIVIL WAR

sible, but afterwards, when all was safe and quiet, I had many a laugh over the way I was to tear about that house while the mob was bursting in the front door, — my husband up in the third story, and I, after pushing the negroes over the fence, scampering about to hide the ladder in some unknown place.

At ten o'clock that evening we were left alone in absolute darkness, as the police sent word that light would increase our danger. John lay quietly on his cot, while I again sat by the window to catch the slightest sound, and in the stillness heard a voice in the adjoining house say, " There 's always a calm before a storm," which, under the circumstances, was not encouraging; I have never forgotten the impression it made on me.

But soon our hearts were gladdened by the sound of the patrol passing our house at regular intervals, and although we were in the third story from the street, the still-

67

LETTERS FROM A SURGEON

ness was so intense that we could distinctly hear their conversation. Suddenly rapid pistol shots broke the spell; then came a great rush up the avenue in the darkness, John's voice saying very calmly, " Here they come." The absolute quiet within us both at the time from its very intensity overpowered all surface emotion. However, the noise proved to be a false alarm, and again came the silence.

Time after time we had these shocks; now the mob seemed almost upon us; then at a distance. What did it mean? Finally the tumult seemed to culminate a block away, and gradually we felt that, for the time at least, our lives were safe. As soon as the strain was over I realized how tense had been my calm, and, as we sat together in the darkness, I must confess to enjoying a comfortable little weep and being much strengthened by it. Such is — myself!

During the night my brothers returned, and told us that just as the officers at the

68

OF THE CIVIL WAR

police station had agreed to combine with the citizens and patrol that vicinity, a man rushed in crying that the mob was murdering some one in our street. The whole force formed and charged up the avenue, but met only scattered bands of rioters, and these slunk away as the files of organized men appeared, stretching in solid lines from sidewalk to sidewalk, as the rioters supposed, fully armed. We heard afterward that this steadfast army, looking so formidable, while so feeble in reality, was all that saved us; that our house and the one opposite, as well as the police station, were distinctly marked by the mob for that night's work.

The ensuing day was still an anxious one, but as it passed and nothing happened, we began to feel at ease again. By this time the city was full of troops, and finally the riot was quelled by firing canister into the mob. As we heard the heavy reports and responding yells, it seemed to me that I

69

LETTERS FROM A SURGEON

knew something of the horrors of war. To-morrow the authorities continue the draft, and I trust they will enforce it in spite of every obstacle.

Before closing this letter, I must tell you of some amusing things which happened when the citizens met at the police station, as related by my brothers on their return, and which even then gave us all a hearty laugh.

They told us that the meeting was a large one, and was called to order at seven o'clock. A vigilance committee was immediately formed for mutual protection, and a chairman and secretary selected. Resolutions were drawn up, various plans were proposed, and among others that of telegraphing to Albany for muskets, — a proposition which a man of some sense suggested was worse than useless, as the mob might be upon them at any moment, reminding them also that the citizens there collected probably knew little of firearms,

70

OF THE CIVIL WAR

so that any guns would be easily seized by the mob and turned against themselves. It was then decided that the citizens could best aid the police by patrolling the streets and reporting at the Station whenever rioters were seen.

A motion was finally made, that in order to know on whom to depend, a list of the names and residences of those present should be taken. This was done with great formality and the loss of much valuable time, each man signing his name, when quite a bombshell was thrown into their midst by the suggestion that spies might be among them. At this the whole assembly seemed to separate one from the other, every man eying his neighbor with sharp suspicion. The secretary, who had been most zealous in calling the meeting, yet whose nervousness was evidently on the increase, suggested in a scarcely audible voice that if the list of names just signed should fall into the hands of the mob, the

71

LETTERS FROM A SURGEON

fate of each member would undoubtedly be sealed. Might it not be wiser, after all, to tear it up?

Great confusion followed these remarks; some laughed; others scoffed; but a terrified exclamation from the poor secretary silenced all. White and shaking, he pointed to the windows, which every one then saw were filled with eager, listening faces. The secretary hesitated no longer, but rushed for the list, tore it in pieces, slammed down the windows, locked the door, and even turned out the lights, before the astonished citizens knew what was happening. Then, when a mad rush for the door was imminent, as the mob outside was preferable to the suffocation and darkness within, a great commotion was heard, — pounding of fists on the door, and shouts to the police that the mob was on its way there, and murdering a man in the next street. The confusion and excitement were indescribable; even the secretary forgot

72

OF THE CIVIL WAR

himself. Each man seized the club which had been provided, and soon the whole force was marching up the avenue.

NOTE. My husband's leave of absence was for ninety days; at the end of that period, being eager to return to his regiment, he left for Washington on crutches. As nothing of importance occurred from the time of the riot until his departure, in September, I once more let his letters speak for themselves.

73

NEW YORK—HANGING AND BURNING A NEGRO IN CLARKSON STREET.

Source: New York City Public Library[10]

NEW YORK—THE RIOT IN LEXINGTON AVENUE.

#20,669 (188?)

Source: New York City Public Library[11]

CHAPTER 5:
RECONSTRUCTION RIOTS

"We regard the Reconstruction Acts (so-called) of Congress as usurpations, and unconstitutional, revolutionary, and void" - Democratic Platform[12]

After the civil war, race relations amongst the citizens worsened. Following Lincoln's assassination, his Vice President, Andrew Johnson became president. Andrew Johnson was a Democrat unlike his predecessor, Abraham Lincoln who was a Republican. Immediately following the war, and prior to Blacks Codes, Blacks exercised their right to vote by voting for the party of "The Great Emancipator", Abraham Lincoln. Oftentimes, their votes would clash with Democratic political motives; and as more Blacks started to vote for Blacks, Blacks were increasing becoming elected officials. White liberal Republicans became incensed by Black who held power and questioned "The White Man's Authority" giving way to an unlikely alliance between Democrats and liberal Republicans called The White League. The White League, founded in Louisiana in 1874 was about the restoral of White Supremacy and called on ALL Whites to regain their power: The statements that follow are an excerpt from their manifesto which was published in newspapers in an effort to get other Whites to join, "Disregarding all minor questions of principle or policy, and having solely in view the maintenance of our hereditary civilization and Christianity menaced by a stupid Africanization, we appeal to men of our race, of whatever language or nationality, to unite with us against that supreme danger."[13]

The White League and The Ku Klux Klan joined forces to terrorize and massacre the Black population and White Radical Republicans. Though Ulysses S. Grant, a Radical Republican, gained the presidency during Reconstruction, his indifference to rioting and reluctance to deploy troops in the Southern States, helped to fuel the power of the White League and the KKK. Their reign of terror served to produce some of the worst massacres in history, including a massacre in Coushatta, the 1866 Riots in Memphis and New Orleans, and the Mississippi riots in Meridian (1871), Vicksburg (1874), and Clinton (1875).

HARPER'S WEEKLY.

JOURNAL OF CIVILIZATION.

Vol. X.—No. 491.]   NEW YORK, SATURDAY, MAY 26, 1866.   [SINGLE COPIES TEN CENTS. $4.00 PER YEAR IN ADVANCE.

THE MEMPHIS RIOTS.

SCENES IN MEMPHIS, TENNESSEE, DURING THE RIOT—BURNING A FREEDMEN'S SCHOOL-HOUSE. [SKETCHED BY A. R. W.]

SCENES IN MEMPHIS, TENNESSEE, DURING THE RIOT—SHOOTING DOWN NEGROES ON THE MORNING OF MAY 2, 1866.—[SKETCHED BY A. R. W.]

Burning a Freedmen's school-house -- Shooting down Negroes on the morning of May 2, 1866 — sketched by A.R.W.[14]

MEMPHIS MASSACRE OF 1866

The leaders of the May 1st,1866 Memphis Riots were the very people expected to protect the population— police officers. There had been long-standing animosity between White police officers and Black military men. The riot in Memphis ended in at least 30 Black people killed and over fifty Black people wounded. The Freedman's Bureau, a governmental agency established to help former slaves who were victims of violence to bring claims against their aggressor, investigated the riot. According to the Freedman's Bureau[15], this riot was the result of an argument over Black people not moving to allow a white police officer to walk on the sidewalk. Sadly, this same excuse was the cause of a riot in Providence, Rhode Island and a riot in Boston on Ann street in 1843. During the riots, Blacks were slaughtered in the streets, women were raped, the police took money from homeowners, burned homes (50), and shot people attempting to escape.

Moreover, the Bureau's report blames local papers which served to anger whites by printing false stories. In the *Reports of the Committees of the House of Representatives During the First Session Thirty- Ninth Congress*[16], citizens of the city furthered this claim. Judge Hunter and Reverend Mr. Tade claim that the press sought to incite the riots by angering whites. The papers that were blamed were the *Memphis Daily Avalanche, The Argus* and *The Ledger*. James Gilbert Ryan in the article "The Memphis Riots of 1866: Terror in a Black Community During Reconstruction"[17] includes a quote from the *Avalanche*,: "the dirty, fanatical, nigger-loving Radicals of this city, who hate the gentlemen of the South because they hold no intercourse with them, and whose equals and companions are the negroes [who] have been here a few years socializing with negroes, educating negroes, and ruining negroes as their chief occupation." Ryan further asserts that the publisher of the paper was also a rioter; and the paper would later welcome the Ku Klux Klan to town. Moreover, the Freedman's Bureau reports that a city official called for the attacks to happen, that others failed to stop the riots, and that there did not seem to be any inclination towards prosecuting those responsible. Unlike most mobs, the perpetrators were not nameless. Many named the people who had killed, maimed and robbed those around them.

What follows is the Bureau's summary of the incidents. Some affidavits have been included. For all affidavits, follow the resource link.
The Freedmen's Bureau Online[18]
Records of the Assistant Commissioner for the State of Tennessee
Bureau of Refugees, Freedmen, and Abandoned Lands, 1865-1869
National Archives Microfilm Publication M999, roll 34
"Reports of Outrages, Riots and Murders, Jan. 15, 1866 - Aug. 12, 1868"

_____

Memphis, Tenn. May 22 '66 Maj.
Genl. O. O. Howard
Commissioner B. R. F. & A. L.
Washington, D. C.
General,

In accordance with the instructions contained in S. O. No. 64, Ex. II, War Dept., B. R. F. & A. L. dated Washington, D. C. May 7, 1866 and your letter of "confidential instructions" of the same date, I have the honor herewith to submit a report of an investigation of the late riots in Memphis.

I reached Memphis May 11th and I found General Fisk, the Asst. Commissioner for Ky. And Tenn. here. He had already directed his Inspector General Col. C. T. Johnson to institute an investigation and I found the Colonel had commenced his work and was well advanced.

At the suggestion of General Fisk I immediately conferred with Colonel Johnson and we determined to make a joint investigation and report. We have taken some affidavits and as many more could have been procured if we could have taken the time.

I have the honor to be

Very Respectfully Your

Obdt. Servant (sd) T.

W. Gilbreth Aid-de-

Camp

Report of an investigation of the cause, origin, and results of the late riots in the city of Memphis made by Col. Charles F. Johnson, Inspector General States of Ky. And Tennessee and Major T. W. Gilbreth, A. D. C. To Maj. Genl. Howard, Commissioner Bureau R. F. & A. Lands.

The remote cause of the riot as it appears to us is a bitterness of feeling which has always existed between the low whites & blacks, both of whom have long advanced rival claims for superiority, both being as degraded as human beings can possibly be.

In addition to this general feeling of hostility there was an especial hatred among the city police for the Colored Soldiers, who were stationed here for a long time and had recently been discharged from the service of the U. S., which was most cordially reciprocated by the soldiers.

This has frequently resulted in minor affrays not considered worthy of notice by the authorities. These causes combined produced a state of feeling between whites and blacks, which would require only the slightest provocation to bring about an open rupture.

The Immediate Cause

On the evening of the 30th April 1866 several policemen (4) came down Causey Street, and meeting a number of Negroes forced them off the sidewalk. In doing so a Negro fell and a policeman stumbled over him. The police then drew their revolvers and attacked the Negroes, beating them with their pistols. Both parties then separated, deferring the settlement by mutual consent to some future time (see affidavit marked "Λ"). On the following day, May 1st, during the afternoon, between the hours of 3 and 5, a crowd of colored men, principally discharged soldiers, many of whom were more or less intoxicated, were assembled on South Street in South Memphis.

Three or four of these were very noisy and boisterous. Six policemen appeared on South Street, two of them arrested two of the Negroes and conducted them from the ground. The others remained behind to keep back the crowd, when the attempt was made by several Negroes to rescue their comrades. The police fell back when a promiscuous fight was indulged in by both parties.

During this affray one police officer was wounded in the finger, another (Stephens) was shot by the accidental discharge of his pistol in his own hand, and afterward died.

About this time the police fired upon unoffending Negroes remote from the riotous quarter. Colored soldiers with whom the police first had trouble had returned in the meantime to Fort Pickering. The police was soon reinforced and commenced firing on the colored people, men, women and children, in that locality, killing and wounding several.

Shortly after, the City Recorder (John C. Creighton) arrived upon the ground (corner of Causey and Vance Streets) and in a speech which received three hearty cheers from the crowd there assembled, councilled and urged the whites to arm and kill every Negro and drive the last one from the city. Then during this night the Negroes were hunted down by police, firemen and other white citizens, shot, assaulted, robbed, and in many instances their houses searched under the pretense of hunting for concealed arms, plundered, and then set on fire, during which no resistance so far as we can learn was offered by the Negroes.

A white man by the name of Dunn, a fireman, was shot and killed by another white man through mistake (reference is here made to accompanying affidavit mkd "B").
During the morning of the 2nd inst. (Wednesday) everything was perfectly quiet in the district of the disturbances of the previous day. A very few Negroes were in the streets, and none of them appeared with arms, or in any way excited except through fear. About 11 o'clock A. M. a posse of police and citizens again appeared in South Memphis and commenced an indiscriminate attack upon the Negroes, they were shot down without mercy, women suffered alike with the men, and in several instances little children were killed by these miscreants. During this day and night, with various intervals of quiet, the nuisance continued.

The city seemed to be under the control of a lawless mob during this and the two succeeding days (3rd & 4th). All crimes imaginable were committed from simple larceny to rape and murder. Several women and children were shot in bed. One woman (Rachel Johnson) was shot and then thrown into the flames of a burning house and consumed. Another was forced twice through the flames and finally escaped. In some instances, houses were fired and armed men guarded them to prevent the escape of those inside. A number of men whose loyalty is undoubted, long residents of Memphis, who deprecated the riot during its progress, were denominated Yankees and Abolitionists, and were informed in language more emphatic than gentlemanly, that their presence here was unnecessary. To particularize further as to individual acts of inhumanity would extend the report to too great a length. But attention is respectfully called for further instances to affidavits accompanying marked C, E, F & G.

The riot lasted until and including the 4th of May but during all this time the disturbances were not continual as there were different times of greater or less length in each day, in which the city was perfectly quiet, attacks occurring generally after sunset each day.
The rioters ceased their violence either of their own accord or from want of material to work on, the Negroes having hid themselves, many fleeing into the country.
Conduct of the Civil Authorities
The Hon. John Park, Mayor of Memphis, seemed to have lost entire control of his subordinates and either through lack of inclination and sympathy with the mob, or on utter want of capacity, completely failed to suppress the riot and preserve the peace of the city. His friends offer in

extenuation of his conduct, that he was in a state of intoxication during a part or most of the time and was therefore unable to perform the high and responsible functions of his office. Since the riot no official notice has been taken of the occurrence either by the Mayor or the Board of Aldermen, neither have the City Courts taken cognizance of the numerous crimes committed.

Although many of the perpetrators are known, no arrests have been made, nor is there now any indication on the part of the Civil Authorities that any are meditated by them.
It appears the Sheriff of this County (P. M. Minters) endeavored to oppose the mob on the evening of the 1st of May, but his good intentions were thwarted by a violent speech delivered by John C. Creighton, City Recorder, who urged and directed the arming of the whites and the wholesale slaughter of blacks.

This speech was delivered on the evening of the 1st of May to a large crowd of police and citizens on the corner of Vance and Causey streets, and to it can be attributed in a great measure the continuance of the disturbances. The following is the speech as extracted from the affidavits herewith forwarded marked "B" . . . " That everyone of the citizens should get arms, organize and go through the Negro districts," and that he "was in favor of killing every God damned nigger" . . . "We are not prepared now, but let us prepare and clean out every damned son of a bitch of a nigger out of town . . . "Boys, I want you to go ahead and kill every damned one of the nigger race and burn up the cradle."

The effect of such language delivered by a municipal office so high in authority, to a promiscuous and excited assemblage can be easily perceived. From that time they seemed to act as though vested with full authority to kill, burn and plunder at will. The conduct of a great number of the city police, who are generally composed of the lowest class of whites selected without reference to their qualifications for the position, was brutal in the extreme. Instead of protecting the rights of persons and property as is their duty, they were chiefly concerned as murderers, incendiaries and robbers. At times they even protected the rest of the mob in their acts of violence.

No public meeting has been held by the citizens, although three weeks have now elapsed since the riot, thus by their silence appearing to approve of the conduct of the mob. The only regrets that are expressed by the mass of the people are purely financial. There are, however, very many honorable exceptions, chiefly among men who have fought against the Government in the late rebellion, who deprecate in strong terms, both the Civil Authorities and the rioters.
Action of Bvt. Brig. Genl. Ben P. Runkle, Chief Supt., Bureau R. F. and A. L., Sub-District of Memphis.

General Runkle was waited upon every hour in the day during the riot, by colored men who begged of him protection for themselves and families, and he, an officer of the Army detailed as Agent of the Freedmen's Bureau was suffered the humiliation of acknowledging his utter inability to protect them in any respect. His personal appearance at the scenes of the riot had no affect on the mob, and he had no troops at his disposal.

He was obliged to put his Headquarters in a defensive state, and we believe it was only owing to the preparations made, that they were not burned down. Threats had been openly made that the Bureau office would be burned, and the General driven from the town. He, with his officers and a small squad of soldiers and some loyal citizens who volunteered were obliged to remain there during Thursday and Friday nights.

The origin and results of the riot may be summed up briefly as follows:
The remote cause was the feeling of bitterness which as always existed between the two classes.
The minor affrays which occurred daily, especially between the police and colored persons.
The general tone of certain city papers which in articles that have appeared almost daily, have councilled the low whites to open hostilities with the blacks.

The immediate cause was the collision heretofore spoken of between a few policemen and Negroes on the evening of the 30th of April in which both parties may be equally culpable, followed on the evening of the 1st May by another collision of a more serious nature and subsequently by an indiscriminate attack upon inoffensive colored men and women.

Three Negro churches were burned, also eight (8) school houses, five (5) of which belonged to the United States Government, and about fifty (50) private dwellings, owned, occupied or inhabited by freedmen as homes, and in which they had all their personal property, scanty though it be, yet valuable to them and in many instances containing the hard earnings of months of labor.
Large sums of money were taken by police and others, the amounts varying five (5) to five hundred (500) dollars, the latter being quite frequent owing to the fact that many of the colored men had just been paid off and discharged from the Army.

No dwellings occupied by white men exclusively were destroyed and we have no evidence of any white men having been robbed.

From the present disturbed condition of the freedmen in the districts where the riot occurred it is impossible to determine the exact number of Negroes killed and wounded. The number already ascertained as killed is about (30) thirty; and the number wounded about fifty (50). Two white men were killed, viz., Stephens, a policemen and Dunn of the Fire Department.

The Surgcon who attended Stephens gives it as his professional opinion that the wound which resulted in his death was caused by the accidental discharge of a pistol in his hands (see affidavit marked "B"). Dunn was killed May 1st by a white man through mistake (see affidavit marked "B"). Two others (both Policemen) were wounded, one slightly in the finger, the other (Slattersly) seriously.

The losses sustained by the Government and Negroes as per affidavits received up to date amount to the sum of ninety eight thousand, three hundred and nineteen dollars and fifty five cents ($98,319.55). Subsequent investigations will in all probability increase the amount to one hundred and twenty thousand dollars ($120,00.00).
(signed) Chas. F. Jackson

Col. And Insptr. Genl. Ky. & Tenn.
T. W. Gilbreth
Aide-de-Camp.

Silas S. Garrett - affidavit - states that he saw the commencement of the riot on 2nd day. Knows the policemen to blame. Has seen their brutal conduct toward black men for the past 12 months.

Before me personally appeared the undersigned who being duly sworn deposes as follows:
My name is Silas S. Garrett, late 1st Lt. 5th U. S. C. Infty. (Heavy). I was with my regiment at Fort Pickering at the time riot commenced. I have reason to believe there were few soldiers away from camp at that time. When it became known that the police were shooting inoffensive blacks in South Memphis, it was with great difficulty that the officers were able to restrain the men from joining in the riot. The guns having been turned over, there was nothing to be done but by moral suasion.
I staid up until a late hour using my best efforts to keep the men in camp.

The next morning, I rode over to South Memphis and saw two of the soldiers that had been killed. From the position in which their bodies laid it was evident that they were trying to get away. This was about 8 O'clock a.m. Everything was quiet in South Memphis at that time. I rode into the city and in about an hour saw a force of policemen (say 15 or 20) under the command of Chief of Police B. G. Garrett - proceeded by 4 or 5 men on horseback and followed by a crowd of excited citizens going in the direction of South Memphis. I followed them down and watched their motions closely.

I saw a policeman pick up a stone and order a black woman to go in the house. She was standing quietly in her own door saying nothing and doing nothing. They arrived at South Memphis and crossed to the opposite side among some shanties occupied by the colored people. I rode immediately to where I could have a full view. There was no disturbance at all.
The police pointed out two or three Negroes and started after them, pistols in hand. The blacks seeing this force, attempted to get away, when the whole force, Police & citizens, began an indiscriminating shooting of inoffensive blacks. I saw one shot and killed as he was moving toward the police with an evident intention of giving himself up. I saw another who had been quietly at work in the yard pursued and killed.

The policemen in this case must have been drunk for he shot at least 4 times at this man within five steps of him without bringing him down. He finally got near enough to knock him down with his pistol.

Soon after, seeing the colored soldiers coming out of the Fort, I rode to the little eminence in rear of the Miss. & Tenn. R. R. Depot and while urging the men to return to their quarters a ball passed in close proximity to my head. I know if it had not been for the police there would have been no row on the 2nd May and but for the brutality of the Irish police towards the blacks as mentioned by myself for the past 12 months in the city of Memphis, there would have been no difficulty at all. (signed) S. S. Garrett

Subscribed and sworn to before me this 14th day of May 1866.
(sgd) Mich. Walsh
Capt. & A. A. A. G.
& Pro. Mar. Freedmen

Affidavit B. Before me personally appeared the undersigned James Cannon Mitchell who upon being duly sworn deposes and says.

My name is James Cannon Mitchell. I am a discharged soldier and live in the city of Memphis, State of Tenn. on River Street near South. I have been a slave and previous to my enlistment in the Federal Army was a servant in the employ of two officers in the rebel army. On the 1st day of May 1866 I was standing in my yard in front of my residence when I saw John Pendergass (white) with two Derringers in his hand and with them he shot a man on Rayburn Avenue. He was a white man and a fireman of the Engine near the "Gayaso House." He (Pendergass) said "God damn it I am sorry I shot this man, I thought he was a God damn yeller nigger." Immediately after Pendergass turned and called a soldier who was running away to come back that he would not hurt him. The soldier came back and Pendergass shot him dead. On the 2nd of May while near my house I saw Roach (a policeman) hit a colored soldier with his revolver, the soldier warded off the blow and Roach then shot him, he (the soldier) falling, when Roach & Jim Halloway started after another soldier and in coming near him, ordered him to halt, he disregarded the order and continued to run. When they ceased pursuing and returned to the other who was wounded (he was wounded so badly that he could not stand) when Jim Halloway shot him unto death.
I saw Cash with the party and saw him firing with them.

James (X) Cannon Mitchell
Subscribed and sworn to before me this the 19th day of May 1866.
F. M. H. Kendrick
Capt. & Asst . Inspt. Genl.

THE REPORTS OF THE COMMITTEES OF THE HOUSE OF REPRESENTATIVES MADE DURING THE FIRST SESSION THIRTY-NINTH CONGRESS
This is an abridged copy showing just some of the atrocities reported.

Brutal MURDER OF JACKSON GOODELL.

Among the first victims to the bloodthirsty spirit of the mob on Tuesday night was Jackson Goodell, a drayman, in no way connected with the soldiers. Coming home from his work at the close of the day, at the request of his wife, who was sick, he went out of the house to a store to get some meal for supper. As he was going into the store, two policemen came out of a grocery next door, and followed him with revolvers. To get away from them he slipped through the house and came out at another door. These policemen saw him and caught him, called him " a d — d rascal," and knocked him down his head falling in the gutter. They struck him fifteen or twenty times, the testimony being that any one of the blows would have killed almost any white man. Then they shot him after he was down. His wife was soon after notified that her husband was killed. She went out and found him on the ground groaning. She pressed her hand to his breast and called him, but " he never spoke." The people in the neighborhood were so frightened at the demonstrations of the mob that none of them dared aid her in bringing him into the house, and she was finally advised that she had better go in or she would be killed, for the policemen were going to kill every negro they could catch. While she was sitting by her wounded husband holding his head in her hands, three policemen came along, and one of them said, " Here is a d — d nigger; if he is not dead, we will finish him." She went out in the morning, but he was not there, and she was afterwards informed that four men had taken him off in the night and was advised that she had better go to the station-house and see about it. She went, and after much difficulty she was enabled, by peeping through the bars of the window, to see her husband lying there dead. With a refinement of cruelty, the station-house keeper refused to allow her to go inside, and also refused to give up the body to her for burial, although she begged for it in the most piteous terms. The testimony of Lavinia Goodell as to this murder is corroborated by that of John E. Moller, who states that he saw them knock down the negro man, and that in the crowd was a policeman on horseback, who was a sergeant or lieutenant, and who said, " Kill them altogether; the God d — d niggers ought to be all killed, no matter whether the small or big ones."

Page 13: REPORTS OF RAPE:
The crowning acts of atrocity and diabolism committed during these terrible nights were the ravishing of five different colored women by these fiends in human shape, independent of other attempts at rape. The details of these out rages are of too shocking and disgusting a character to be given at length in this report, and reference must be had to the testimony of the parties. It is a singular fact, that while this mob was breathing vengeance against the negroes and shooting them down like dogs, yet when they found unprotected colored women they at once "conquered their prejudices," and proceeded to violate them under circumstances of the most licentious brutality.

FRANCES THOMPSON. The rape of Frances Thompson, who had been a slave and was a cripple, using crutches, having a cancer on her foot, is one to which reference is here made. On Tuesday night seven men, two of whom were policemen, came to her house. She knew the two to be policemen by their stars. They were all Irishmen. They first demanded that she should get supper for them, which she did. After supper the wretches threw all the provisions that were in the house which had not been consumed out into the bayou. They then laid hold of Frances, hitting her on the side of the face and kicking her. A girl by the name of Lucy Smith, about sixteen years old, living with her, attempted to go out at the window. One of the brutes knocked her down and choked her. They then drew their pistols, and said they would shoot them and fire the house if they did not let them have their way. The woman, Frances Thompson, was then violated by four of the men, and so beaten and bruised that she lay in bed for three days. They then took all the clothes out of the trunk, one hundred dollars in greenbacks belonging to herself, and two hundred dollars belonging to another colored woman, which had been left to take care of her child, besides silk dresses, bed- clothing, &c. They were in the house nearly four hours, and when they left they said they intended " to burn up the last God damned nigger, and drive all the Yankees out of town, and then there would be only some rebel niggers and butternuts left."

The colored girl, Lucy Smith, who was before the committee, said to be sixteen or seventeen years old, but who seemed, from her appearance, to be two or three years younger, was a girl of modest demeanor and highly respectable in appearance. She corroborated the testimony of Frances Thompson as to the number of men who broke into the house and as to the policemen who were with them. They seized her (Lucy) by the neck and choked her to such an extent that she could not talk for two weeks to anyone. She was then violated by one of the men, and the reason given by another for not repeating the act of nameless atrocity was, that she was so near dead he would not have anything to do with her. He there upon struck her a severe blow upon the side of the head. The violence of these wretches seemed to be aggravated by the fact that the women had in their room some bed-covering or quilting with red, white, and blue, and also some picture of Union officers. They said, " You niggers have a mighty liking for the damned Yankees, but we will kill you, and you will have no liking for any one then." This young girl was so badly injured that she was unable to leave her bed for two weeks.

Page 15: SHOOTING AND BURNING OF RACHAL HATCHER.

The shooting and burning of a colored girl by the name of Rachel Hatcher was one of the most cruel and bloody acts of the mob. This girl Rachel was about sixteen years of age. She was represented by all to be a girl of remark able intelligence, and of pure and excellent character. She attended school, and such had been her proficiency that she herself had become a teacher of the smaller scholars. Her mother, Jane Sneed, testified before the committee that on Tuesday night the mob came to her house, took a man out, took him down to the bridge and shot him." They then set fire to the house of an old colored man by the name of Adam Lock, right by the house of the witness. Her daughter, Rachel, seeing the house of a neighbor on fire, proposed to go and help get the things out. While in the house, engaged in an act of benevolent heroism, the savages surrounded the burning building, and with loaded revolvers threatened to shoot her. In piteous tones she implored them to let her come out ; but one of the crowd — the wretch Pendergrast — said, " No ; if you don't go back I will blow your damned brains out." As the flames gathered about her she emerged from the burning house, when the whole crowd " fired at her as fast as they could." She was deliberately shot, and fell dead between the two houses. Her clothes soon took fire, and her body was partially consumed, presenting a spectacle horrible to behold. The mother of Rachel was, in the meantime, inside her own house trying to get out a man who was wounded that night, and who she was afraid would be burnt up. When she came back she saw the dead body of her daughter, the blood running out of her mouth. There was an Irishman about her house at this time by the name of Callahan, with the largest pistol in his hand she had ever seen. He demanded that her husband should come out until he could shoot him. But his life was saved at that moment by the appearance of two regulars, who told them to go to the fort.

Anna George - affidavit - states that on 1st May '66 she witnessed an encounter between police & discharged col'd soldiers - that Chief shot 3 of soldiers dead - next day saw white men kill 2 more soldiers - afire a school house - also throw a wounded girl into the flames & fired on her mother when interceding on her daughter's behalf.

Before me personally appeared the undersigned Anna George and being duly sworn deposes as follows:

My name is Anna George. I live in Memphis, Tenn. On South St. near Mr. Ryan's grocery. On the 1st of May 1866 while standing at the door of the Ryan's grocery I saw a big fat Policeman called "Reddy" attempt to arrest a soldier for being drunk. The other soldiers prevented the arrest. The officer then left and said "I'll see you before daylight" and went to Causey St. where there were several white policemen. After joining the policemen alluded to and holding a few moments conversation with them, they all returned towards the colored men who ran towards the Fort and as they were running the police fired a number of shots at them and kept following and firing. I followed and saw three colored men dead, three more shot. Then the col'd men exchanged shots and immediately broke & ran again. I saw "Reddy" & "Johnson" (policemen) firing at the colored men.

On the next morning the 2nd I saw a number of white men shoot and kill two colored soldiers who were passing along quietly attending to their own business. I then saw the mob fire the col'd school house at the corner of South & Causey Sts. and also bring furniture out of the houses of colored people and throw it into the fire. The houses were owned by white people. In the evening they set fire to the houses and I went to see it.
I saw the girl Frances Johnson who was shot and groaning, her mother was upbraiding the mob when they took the girl who was still alive and threw her into the fire and shot at her mother who ran away. The girl was burnt to death.

There was quite a number of police with the crowd, they were encouraging them to go on. The police had badges on at the time and did not arrest anyone.
Anna (x) George

Subscribed and sworn to before me at Memphis, Tenn. this 18th day of May 1866.
(sgd) Michl. Walsh
Capt. & A. A. A. G.
& P. M. Freedmen

There are several more first-person reports available via the Congressional Report or the Freedmen's Bureau Report. Since the Freedmen's Bureau Report was made shortly after the crisis, the full scope of injury and destruction could not be ascertained. Page 34 of the Congressional Report offers:

THE RESULTS OF THE RIOT.

The resolution of the House directed the committee to ascertain the number of the killed and wounded, the names of the parties engaged in the riot, and the amount and character of the property destroyed. These facts the committee have ascertained in detail, as far as practicable, and present the following proximate results:

THE KILLED.

The number ascertained by the testimony taken by your committee, in common with that taken by General Stoneman's and the Freedmen's Bureau commission, to have been killed, including the white men Dunn and Stevens, is 48, and the names are given as far as known ; but there is no doubt in the minds of your committee that many persons were killed whose killing has not been proved. A vast number of colored people had come into Memphis and located in this neighborhood, who were but little known, and who, during the progress of the riot, fled in all directions. Nothing was ascertained from them what portion of their number was killed. The following is a list of the killed, as far as could be ascertained by the committee. The names are given as far as known. ' A large number were killed whose names are not known:

COLORED PERSONS KILLED —46

Joseph Lundy, 3d United States colored heavy artillery
Isaac Richardson, 3d United States colored heavy artillery
William Withers, 3d United States colored heavy artillery
George Cobb, 3d United States colored heavy artillery
George Black, 3d United States colored heavy artillery Bob
Taylor, 3d United States colored heavy artillery Lewis
Robinson
Levi Baker George
Williams
Unknown negroman, at Grady's Hill
Unknown negro man, on Mulberry street
William Henry, at corner of Henry and McCall streets
Unknown negro man, on South street, near Mississippi and Tennessee rail road depot
Two colored soldiers, east of the Mississippi and Tennessee railroad depot
Colored soldier, on South street, near Rayburn avenue
Colored soldier, east of South street bridge
George Anderson
Old negro man, south side Beale street, near Second
Two negroes, in the creek south of South street
Unknown negro man, on De Soto street
Unknown negro man
Freeman Jones
Negro boy, on South street.near Causey
Negro woman, Emeline, South street
Colored soldier, corner of Linden and St. Martin streets
Unknown negro man, corner of Shelby and South streets
Rachel Hatcher
Unknown negro man, near intersection of Rayburn avenue and South street.
Colored soldier, at negro quarters, south of South street
William H. Saunders
Colored soldier, on South street
Colored soldier
John Robinson

Two unknown negro men, on road side
Unknown negro boy, on road side
Charley Wallace
Unknown negro man
Shade Long
Adeline Miller
Jackson Goodell
Daniel Hawkins
Uncle Dick Robert
Carlton

Stephens, policeman Dunn, fireman

THE WOUNDED AND MALTREATED.

As near as your committee could ascertain, from their investigations and from the testimony taken by the two commissioners, there were between seventy and eighty persons wounded. Many of them were identified by name, and many were known to be wounded — some severely, some slightly — whose names could not be ascertained, as they had fled from the city. There were some ten or twelve persons in addition to this number who were badly maltreated.

ROBBERIES.

There were one hundred distinct robberies, more or less aggravated. The committee have included in this number the robberies of colored individuals that took place during the entire week in which the riots occurred.

BURNINGS.

As has been stated, four churches and twelve school-houses were burned, and the number of other houses and cabins burnt was in the neighborhood of ninety.

PROPERTY DESTROYED.

It has been difficult to ascertain the precise amount of property destroyed. Your committee took much testimony in regard to that subject, but less than that taken by the Freedmen's Bureau commission, whose investigations on this branch of the subject are perhaps fuller than that taken by any other. That commission reports that the loss sustained by the government and the negroes, up to the date of making their report, was $98,319 55; and it was reported that subsequent investigations would increase the amount to at least $120,000. As near as your committee could ascertain from the testimony taken by them and from the other investigations, the amount of government property destroyed was in the neighborhood of $17,000, besides the expenses incurred by General Stoneman, and by the commissary and quartermaster's departments, in the transfer of troops and transportation of persons who left the city in fear of mob violence, amounting in the aggregate to $130,981 41.

NEW ORLEANS MASSACRE OF 1866

The cartoon shows President Andrew Johnson "as a king, crowned and in velvet and ermine. His alleged royalist ambition had been the theme of much Radical rhetoric." The artist, Thomas Nast is attacking Johnson because he and others blamed Johnson for causing the July 1866 race riot that occurred in New Orleans when police shot and killed many African American delegates at a Radical Republicans convention.[19]
It was no Riot— It was an Absolute Massacre by the Police — A Murder Perpetrated by the Mayor "

In New Orleans, on July 30th[th] 1866 there was a large-scale massacre of mostly African American *Radical* Republican, called such due to their "progressive" views of extending rights to all men. African Americans, at this time were Republican, and voted as such as *Radical* White Republicans had been Abolitionists and fought on the side of the Union during the war. Most Southern Democrats were Confederates. When Reconstruction began, African Americans were allowed to vote, but due to the large number of African Americans who voted Republican, many Democrats sought to disenfranchise African Americans through Black Codes. Assertion of rights, particularly the right to vote, was at the heart of many race riots — 1868 in Abbeville County, South Carolina, the riot occurred at the polling place, prior to the 1917 Race Riots rumors were spread that Blacks were colonizing the vote, a riot in Mobile Alabama occurred during an election, Wilmington Riot in 1898, Ocoee, Florida Riot of 1919 to name a few. These are several more instances. In 1866,
R.K. Howell, reconvened the Convention of 1864 with the purpose of electing officials to revise and amend the Constitution of Louisiana to assure that all men were given equal rights.

Upon hearing of the reconvening, the President of the United States, Andrew Johnson, wrote a telegram to the Governor of Louisiana.[20]

War Department, July 28, 1866.
To His Excellency Governor Wells:
I have been advised that you have issued a proclamation convening the convention elected in 1864. Please inform me under and by what authority this has been done, and by what authority this convention can assume to represent the whole people of the State of Louisiana.
(Signed) Andrew Johnson.

Governor Wells responded:
STATE OF LOUISIANA.
Executive Department, New Orleans, July 28, 1866.
To His Excellency Andrew Johnson, President of the United States:
Your telegram is received. I have not issued any order convening the convention of 1864. The convention was convened by the president of that body, by virtue of a resolution authorizing him to do so, and in that event for him to call on the proper officers of the State to issue writs of election for delegates in unrepresented parishes. My proclamation was issued in response to that call. As soon as vacancies can be ascertained, they will be filled; and then the whole State will be represented in the convention.
(SIGNED) J. Madison Wells, Governor.

News reports *excited* those on the side of the Union and *incited* those on the side of the Confederate. Reports were of a coup to usurp the authority of the President and the State. The mayor of New Orleans, John T. Monroe, orchestrated the riot. He assured that the military would not intervene with the 'arrests' of those referred to him as an unlawful as an unlawful assembly of men "whose avowed object is to subvert the municipal and State governments." President Johnson was also culpable in the actions of the mob as he not only denounced the groups authority, but also ordered the military not to intervene with the 'arrests' of the member of the Convention. The following is an account from the Library of Congress, which quotes a *New York Times* article.

Newspaper accounts of the riot:

New York Times Report:

I have already forwarded a number of disconnected despatches relative to to-day's fearful carnage, and now propose to give you a more connected account. I only write of what I saw with my own eyes, and which I can substantiate on the best authority.

The convention met at 12 o'clock, 26 members being present, Judge R. K. Howell (since missing) in the chair. R. King Cutler (also missing) moved an adjournment of one hour, during which time the sergeant-at-arms was directed to compel the attendance of absentees. The hall was densely packed with freedmen and whites, the former having armed themselves extensively since their Friday's demonstrations.

Just after the adjournment a procession, containing about a hundred freedmen carrying a United States flag, and marching through the streets with martial music, arrived at the [Mechanics] Institute, having had a slight disturbance on Canal street. At this juncture the merchants all over the city, fearing the coming riot, closed their stores.

When the procession entered the building a squad of police followed, and attempted to make arrests. A scene of the wildest confusion followed. Pistols were fired, clubs and canes-used, and brick-bats flew in every direction. **The policemen claim that they were merely attempting to arrest the Canal-street rioters above mentioned; but certain it is that they mounted the platform, where a small body of the members yet remained, and one of them presented a pistol at them, using offensive language.** The policemen were finally driven out of the building, leaving inside Governor Hahn, Judge Howell, Mr. Dostie, and other gentlemen, mostly clerks attached to the State government, besides about fifty freedmen. Fortunately Governor Wells had just left the building for the purpose of consulting with General Baird about calling out troops, Sheridan being out of town.

The Institute, used now as the State capitol, is located on Dryades street, between Canal and Common, and when the policemen were driven out they were met by a large body of freedmen, who caused them to fall back to Canal street. Hiring a furniture cart, I used it as an observatory on Canal street, looking toward Common through Dryades. The policemen rullied, and drove the freedmen and their friends back to Common, who in turn were driven back to Canal, leaving Dryades perfectly clear of any vestige of humanity, except the bodies of three dead freedmen. Up to this time one police officer had been mortally wounded, one severely, and another slightly hurt with clubs and pistol shots. Police reinforcements soon appeared in Canal street, and the crowd of rioters accompanying the police. The police approached the Institute, and commenced throwing stones through the windows, and firing pistols at any one they could see inside the building. **At the same time a detachment of police attacked the crowd of freedmen on Common street, and after sharp firing, and riddling and wounding several blacks, they drove them away.**

This gave the police and the mob which accompanied them full control of Dryades street. A fire engine was brought out and placed in front of the Institute; for what purpose I do not know. Several attempts were made by the police to enter the building, but they were repulsed. The ammunition of the men in the Institute seemed to give out about this time, as they did not fire any more. They attempted to escape through the rear of the Institute into Baronne street, but were met and either arrested or shot down. They also tried to escape through an alley which runs from Dryades to Baronne street on the Canal-street side. I do not know that any freedmen succeeded in getting away from the building alive, although I saw several at a distance from it being marched to the police headquarters. **I think that every freedman who tried to escape from it was killed; and I saw several shot in the alley above mentioned, and after they fell I saw crowds of ruffians beating them as they were dying. The policemen, whatever their orders were, behaved well toward the white prisoners, comparatively speaking. A Mr. Fisk was the first conventionist captured; and I am happy to say, that although the police could not prevent the crowd from abusing him badly, they did keep him from being lynched. A man mounted a lamp-post on Canal street as Fisk was being carried by under guard, and got a rope ready to hang him; but the guard drove the crowd away with their pistols.** The next member arrested was Captain Haynes, a Texas scout for our army during the war. The crowd had been taught a lesson, and did not interfere with him, although they grumbled deeply as he passed through, calling them "s—s of b—s," "rebels," "traitors," and other pet names.

Governor Hahn succeeded in getting into the hands of the police unhurt from out of the building, where he had been, not as a member, but as one of the most prominent equal-rights men in the State. While he was under guard, however, some coward shot him through the back of the head, inflicting a dangerous wound, and he was also stabbed. He was then placed in a hack and carried to the police headquarters, where I saw him. He was very pale; blood trickled down his face from a wound which seemed to have reached his left temple. Dr. Dostie, who has the reputation of being the most violent negro suffrage man in the South, and who certainly was the most violent speaker on Friday last, was killed while attempting to get away. I am told that a policeman shot him in the back, and that after he fell a crowd jumped on him and cut him horribly with knives.

John Henderson and other members of the convention were also captured, and were wounded by stray shots, the local papers say, but more likely by cowardly rioters while on their way to the station house.

The riot commenced at a quarter past twelve and ended at half-past three. At a quarter before three the military, under General Baird, appeared on Canal street, and finally took possession of the whole city.

Before night the riot was confined to Dryades, Baronne, Common, Carondelet, and Canal streets, and the building and yards all around the Institute. I saw freedmen shot down on all of the above streets, except Canal, who could have been arrested uninjured.

How many men have been killed, wounded, or even arrested, it is impossible to say; but my estimate is one hundred freedmen and twenty-five whites killed and wounded, and one hundred altogether arrested.

The substantial men of the city deplore the occurrence, but all are very violent in their expressions—some glorying in the murder of Dostie, and others in the murder of the freedmen.

The Cincinnati Commercial

"The mob, backed by the police, are reveling in blood; negroes and Union men are hunted down together.

"Since my last dispatch, I have traversed. Common and Dryades streets, past the capitol. The crowd on Common street was raging in the wildest manner; a negro was seen running, and immediately followed him with a hue and cry, shouting, 'Kill him! shoot him!' He disappeared in a yard behind the capitol. A drunken rowdy swung his revolver and yelled, 'Hurrah for hell! hurrah for Louisiana!' A stout citizen cried, with tears in his eyes and clenched fists, 'It's a shame! it's a shame!'

"On Dryades street the mob had gathered about a trembling white man, saying, 'Hold on there; we've got you now; say, were you in the army or not?' A fire engine plunged into the street, driven by a drunken man, and shouts were heard, 'Fire the Institute,' that is, the capitol, where some of the convention were still at bay, defending their lives.

"Shots, like a skirmish fire, rang all about me. On Canal street I came upon blood on the pavement, and, being beckoned in, found Capt. Burke and also the chief of police wounded.

"A reign of terror broods. Respectable citizens are filled with chagrin and sorrow. The police have been, in every case to which I have been an eye-witness, the supporters and leaders of the mob. No marked Union man dared venture abroad.

" July 30, 7½ P. M. —The massacre is over for the present. It is now understood to have been a concerted plan on the part of the rebels, among whom the President's dispatch was known yesterday morning. At the tap of a fire bell the rioters left their business, having lately purchased revolvers, to meet and be led by the police, who were also armed to the teeth. All rushed to the convention, breaking down the fences on Baronne street, in the rear of the capitol, which was surrounded by a force of police.

"They then ran into the building; and, while the crowd outside were firing into the windows, climbed the stairs inside, their leaders shouting, 'Rally, boys—rally,' and discharged their pistols into the Representative Hall, where there were, at the time, but fifteen conventioners (it being during the recess) within the railing, and about seventy-five negroes in the lobby, all of whom in the hall prostrated themselves to escape the shots. As soon as the pistols of the police were emptied, the besieged rose and drove out the assailants with chairs, at the same time barricading the doors. Then R. King Cutler called upon all those who had arms to leave the hall, and Captain Burke, the gallant chief of police deposed by Monroe, went out and fought his way back to Baronne street, escaping with a shot in the side.

"The fury of the besiegers increased, the barricade was broken, and pistols were again discharged. **Then Rev. Mr. Horton, ex-army chaplain, who had made the prayer at the opening of the convention, advanced to the door, and, showing a white handkerchief, asked for himself and the rest to surrender. He was fired upon, hit by the shot in the forehead, then seized and beaten till he was insensible by the mob and police. One after another the members of the convention in the hall waved their handkerchiefs, protesting that they were unarmed and wished to surrender. Yet not a single arrest was made in the hall, but each man, as he came out, hoping to escape the certain fate threatened him if he remained, was seized and brutally handled by the police.**

"Poor Dostie pleaded for his life. He was a Union exile; but, by his kind treatment to rebel families in the absence of their protectors, he had endeared himself to many even of his political enemies."

The New Orleans Advocate:

Returning from the post office about half-past twelve o'clock on Monday last, in company with Rev. Mr. Jackson, who is one of the assistant editors of this paper, our curiosity led us to look in on the convention, to see what they were doing. We passed up Canal street until we arrived at Liberty street, on which the Mechanics' Institute, the building occupied by the convention, is located; here was a gathering of people, mostly colored; we saw a band of music followed by a procession of colored people coming up Burgundy street toward us. We stopped near the corner to see the number in the procession, which appeared to be comparatively small, as it reached but little, if any, more than across Canal street. As the rear of the procession had come on to this street a pistol shot was heard near the southeast corner of Canal and Burgundy streets. The colored people scattered, thus breaking up the procession; none that we saw, however, running but a rod or two at the moment. One or two of these picked up loose cobble stones to defend themselves, thinking an attack was being made on them. The person firing the pistol went down Canal street, toward the river, and a number of colored people started in that direction. **Thinking that a policeman had attempted to arrest someone at the rear of the procession, and through the individual's refusing to go, or some other reason, he had fired his pistol, we ran among the colored people, some of whom appeared greatly excited, and told them to pay no attention to this affair, but go on to the meeting, and not let it be said to-day that they had any disturbance among them. Two or three instantly sanctioned my remarks, one saying, "yes, we are pledged not to have any disturbance on our part."** This was the substance, if not his exact words. **We also remarked to several persons in different parts of the crowd, that if the police arrested any of their people, to make no attempt to rescue them, for they would only be taken to the station house at most, and if not guilty of any offense they would be discharged, but if they attempted to rescue them, it would create a disturbance. To this all seemed to acquiesce.**

They came on then toward the Mechanics' Institute, but a half block distant. Soon there arrived a tall young colored man, who it seems was the person fired at. We went up to him and asked if he was hurt, and who shot at him. He replied that he was not hurt enough to amount to anything, that the ball only grazed his leg, at the same time pointing with his cane to his pants, which appeared to have received some injury. He replied that it was a white fellow that fired, and then ran; that he was not far distant when he fired; that he desired and endeavored to arrest him; that he struck at him with his cane, which he then had in his hand, but that he did not hit him, and that he had got away.

Supposing that the difficulty was all over, we went into the building. The convention, it seemed, had been opened by prayer by Rev. Mr. Horton, but it appeared that there was not a quorum present, at least there was no business being attended to, but the people were in groups around the room, quietly engaged in conversation. As we were glancing about to see who were there, the firing of pistols commenced outside. Shots were fired in rapid succession. Many of the colored people who were nearest the doors rushed down stairs to see what was the matter; others ran to the side windows where they could get a partial view of the street, there being no front window on this floor from which they could see the street. We went to the head of the stairs, but they were so crowded that, instead of going down, we went up one flight of stairs higher, where we could look down from front windows into the street below. **We could there see the policemen firing large revolvers rapidly into the small crowd of colored people around the door below. Other people were hurling bricks at them, and also hurling them at the windows of the room in which the convention was assembled. Occasionally we heard a shot fired from the door below, and saw two or three, perhaps more, bricks hurled towards the police. We saw one colored man lying dead on the opposite side-walk. One colored man only remained anywhere near on that side. Just as we looked out he, a man apparently well along in years, was walking moderately along, and had arrived within twenty or thirty feet of a police officer, when the latter leveled his revolver at him and fired. The poor man fell on his face, apparently dead. A citizen near the policeman, one of the ' chivalry, ' we suppose, not wishing to be out-done in fiendishness, threw a half brick at the head of the colored man after he fell on the pavement.** As the police and the rest of the rioters were well armed, and as but very few of the colored people had come prepared for such an attack, of course the latter were quickly dispersed, though several by this time had been killed and wounded. We saw a federal officer, alone, exerting himself to the utmost to persuade the police and others to go away from the place. They retired half a block to Canal street, either because there were no more in front of the building to shoot at or to consult as to what they should do next. They were hooting and yelling every minute or two. There need have been no bloodshed after this, as now no one was molesting or opposing them. They were clearly the masters of the field. But no, their bloody programme was but just commenced. From our position we could see that they were rather beyond pistol range, and as the firing had all ceased, fearing that an attack might be made on the building, we concluded to leave. As we passed down they were just shutting and fastening the door leading into the room occupied by the convention. It was too late now to attempt to find our friend, from whom we had become separated when the firing commenced. We therefore passed on out of the building and walked rapidly in the opposite direction from the crowd towards Common street. We had gone but a few rods when they raised another yell, and, looking around, we saw they were rushing towards the building. As they were advancing we walked as rapidly as possible till, reaching Common street, we turned the corner and then ran up Common to Baronne.

When near the latter street we knew by the yelling that a portion of the rioters were coming up that street also and stepped into the office on the corner and let them pass by. They now had the building and even the square in which it was located surrounded. We then stepped out the front door on to Baronne street and hastened away from the vicinity. At the headquarters of General Baird we received information that orders had been sent for the colored regiment, in the upper part of the city, to report for duty, and soon learned that orders to the same effect had been sent to the white regiment at Jackson Barracks, below the city. There was considerable delay in their arrival, owing to the distance, and perhaps some other reasons, so that when they arrived the bloody work was about finished.
After the mob had surrounded the building, they fired at any one who appeared at the windows, or who endeavored to leave the building.
Our friend Rev. H. G. Jackson, who was within, and who was severely wounded, states to us that just before the first entrance of the police into the room, Dr. Dostie and R. K. Cutler, who were on the platform, called on the crowd to sit down and offer no resistance. They obeyed, and about twelve policemen then entered, ranged themselves in line, leveled their

pistols, and commenced firing. The negroes immediately jumped up and fled affrighted to the platform. The police fired two or three volleys direct on the convention, when the members rallied, and by chairs and other means drove them back, but only when they found they were to be shot down after their surrender. We saw but few pistols used by members of the convention.

After three attempts the police effected a permanent entrance. Those within not being able to offer further resistance to the greatly increased force brought against them, could only surrender unconditionally. And such was their course.

They waved their white handkerchiefs, exclaiming, "We surrender, we surrender!" But like their infernal companions at Fort Pillow, and elsewhere in the late war, to anything but savage barbarity they were strangers.

They shot, clubbed, and stabbed indiscriminately. Some, among whom was Rev. Mr. Jackson, referred to above, were told by the policemen within to pass out. As soon as Mr. Jackson reached the stairs policemen and citizens assaulted him. He was immediately knocked down with clubs and then shot through the body. The ball entered the right side, and passing through both lungs, came out under the left arm. He is still living, and strong hopes are entertained of his recovery. But like all those who were wounded, and those who were not, he was taken to the police station and locked in a cell. His name was not recorded among the list of prisoners, and though we went to the 10 station house twice, we were informed that he was not there. And it was not until about nine o'clock at night that Dr. Avery, who had gained access to the cells, found him in his sad condition, and succeeded in obtaining his release. And to him too many thanks cannot be awarded. Rev. Mr. Horton, formerly of Boston, who was present and opened the convention with prayer, was shot through the arm, the ball entering his side and lodging, it is thought, in his lung. His head was horribly beaten and cut, and the skull fractured. There are two or three holes in his right cheek, but whether from pistol shots or not we have not heard. One of his fingers is also broken. He has been sensible only a short time since he was hurt, and it is not expected that he will live.

Mr. Fish, a young lawyer here, of an excellent mind and heart, informed us that he succeeded in reaching the sidewalk before getting knocked down. He hastened to a policeman near, and surrendering himself, desired to be taken prisoner that he might be protected. But the brute struck him on the head with a heavy revolver and knocked him down. He gathered up as quickly as possible, and hastened toward another police officer in the middle of the road to surrender himself and get protection, but this one, more villainous still, leveled his revolver at him. He turned and started to run toward Common street. But the policeman's shot took effect in the back of his head, inflicting a horrible wound. He was also shot in the back and arm, and terribly beaten. One or two police, however, finally took charge of him and led him away. But we will not give each man's account separately, as the military commission that has been ordered will collect their statements, and they will probably be published.

Among those seriously wounded of the whites, besides those mentioned above, are ex-Governor Hahn, Mr. Shaw, Mr. Henderson, Dr. Hire, Dr. Dostie, and many others. A lieutenant who was mustered out of the United States service a few days previous, and who was appointed by the convention sergeant-at-arms, was killed outright. Some of those mentioned above will probably die, as some of them have received so many and such severe wounds.

The colored people fared much worse. There were killed of these about forty or fifty, we judge, and probably nearly two hundred wounded—mostly shot. After General Baird had proclaimed martial law, on Monday evening, all those persons arrested in connection with the convention were released from the police station, and the wounded were sent to the Marine Hospital as rapidly as transportation could be furnished them. Some of them, however, were dead when they reached there. This number has since been increased to about one hundred and twenty-five. The Times says about thirty dead bodies lay in the street near the Mechanics' Institute at one time, just as the riot had ceased. Some were killed in the house and at other places also.

The Bee (excerpts from the report)

The small number of the mayor's party killed and the great slaughter on the other side shows plainly that those interested in the convention expected no difficulty, and were therefore not prepared for defense, while there is ample testimony, which will be produced, to show that the murderous attack on the convention had been previously planned.

The most horrible brutality was manifested in the boasting of some of the murderers, as well as in their actions. One man boasted of having killed three "niggers" with an axe. As one of those taken to the city hospital has had his skull cleaved open with an axe, and one side pried up, we suppose that this is one of this boaster's victims. We suppose that the information that one of these still lives will lessen the enjoyment of the fiend, as perhaps he can now boast of having fully murdered only two.

One was heard to boast that six Yankee ministers had been killed by them. It may be a source of grief to them to know that there were only two, and those are not yet dead. The morning after the riot individuals were heard to make inquiry of their friends as to how many niggers they had killed the day previous.

We saw one young mulatto man, near headquarters, before the riot was over, who had escaped from the vicinity and who was crying with mingled sorrow and rage. He said that he was assisting a wounded colored man away, and a young boy came up and putting a pistol to the man's breast fired it, and the man dropped from him dead. Many of those severely wounded were thrown into carts as carelessly as they would handle the dead bodies of swine. But we will not continue these horrid accounts further, though many of the most heart-rending cases we have not yet related, but will endeavor to do so in another issue.

The mayor, … and his gang, it is thought, had fully agreed beforehand on the part they would perform, and it seems that the fire alarm was to be the signal that the war had commenced. The fire-bell rang, and the firemen and the rest of the "special police" were quickly on hand to participate.

Telegram on August 2nd 1866 written by U. S. Grant, General, Washington, D. C.:

The more information I obtain of the affair of the 30th, in this city, the more revolting it becomes. It was not riot; it was an absolute massacre by the police, which was not excelled in murderous cruelty by that of Fort Pillow. It was a murder which the mayor and police of the city perpetrated without the shadow of a necessity. Furthermore, I believe it was premeditated, and every indication points to this. I recommend the removal of this bad man. I believe it would be hailed with the sincerest gratification by two-thirds of the population of the city. There has been a feeling of insecurity on the part of the people here, on account of this man, which is now so much increased, that the safety of life and property does not rest with the civil authorities, but with the military.

Major General Baird's final report: "The Police could have suppressed the Riot had they not been the Rioters."

New Orleans would suffer two more devastating riots in 1901 and 1920. In Charleston, South Carolina a riot occurred in August. One White man died and several were injured.[21] There would be another riot in Charleston during the Red Summer of 1919.

1871 MERIDIAN MISSISSIPPI[22]

JACKSON, MISS., March 9, 1871,
Received March 19, 12 m.

HON. SENATOR AMES, Senate Chamber:

The Meridian riot seems, from information by most reliable persons. to have been the result of a combined effort of the whites to overthrow the city and county government. Result is eight or more colored persons killed. Bramlette, white man. killed by accidental shot. Serators Gleed and Henderson. members, arrived by train from Meridian this p. m., report colored men lying out hidden in the woods, whites patrolling the streets. trains and surrounding country armed. Large Republican caucus earnestly urge on Congress the necessity of prompt and thorough measures to suppress outrage and violence in all parts of the State.

H. W. WARREN,
President Republican Caucus.

1875 CLINTON, MISSISSIPPI RIOTS

In the 1871 Meridian riots, the first report in a Southern newspaper had that a Black man, Warren Tyler, entered a courtroom where he was being charged. He then shot and killed the judge. Later reports and trial testimony would prove that these accounts were false. Reports of this nature were often used by newspapers to further anger the local population and justify riots to the national population. Author, Boston and Columbia University Lecturer, Terry Ann Knopf, in the article "Race, Riots and Reporting" stated:

> Based upon a survey of the riots studied, the writer found many glaring instances of misreporting by the press—spanning both world wars, encompassing every section of the country, and including newspapers large and small, supposedly liberal and conservative. Generally speaking, this misreporting took the form of one-sided, biased, and distorted press coverage against blacks, reflecting and exploiting the sentiments of the white community. An initial inspection of the data revealed four themes: a receptiveness to many rumors circulating among whites that were hostile in content and directed against blacks; unwarranted and unnecessary attacks on blacks which continually placed them in an unfavorable light; the use of loaded language when describing or referring to blacks [describing the race as prone to criminality]; and a rigid adherence to the white version of events.[23]

For the Clinton Riots, these two newspaper articles can show how disparate news reporting frequently were. Both reports are reprinted in the September 7th, 1875 edition of *The Philadelphia Inquirer.*[24]

THE MISSISSIPPI RIOT.

A Clearer Statement of the Troubles at Clinton.

VICKSBURG, Miss., Sept. 6.—An extra edition of the *Herald* gives the following account of the disturbance at Clinton:—The origin and particulars of the riot at Clinton Saturday afternoon have been variously stated. After hearing all the statements we think the following about correct:—There is a law prohibiting the sale of liquor in Clinton. Some young men from Raymond brought a bottle with them, and while the speaking was going on Martin Siveley and some of his friends went off a short distance to take a drink. The colored marshal for the occasion approached them and forbade the drinking.

This order was not regarded, and when the marshal attempted to take the bottle from Siveley's hand Siveley struck him over the head with it. Senator Caldwell, colored, started to settle the difficulty, and was followed by some twenty negroes, whom he ordered back, but about a hundred more came rushing on. Some one fired a shot, which was followed by a general firing and a stampede. Siveley fired all the barrels of his pistol, and the negroes then demanded his surrender. He surrendered and gave up his pistol, after which he was shot and his brains knocked out. He was then robbed of his clothing, and a finger was cut off in order to get his ring.

The infuriated mob found Charles Chilton in his yard and shot and killed him in the presence of his family. Frank Thomasson, a promising young lawyer, was shot from his house a mile and a half from the scene of the conflict, and after falling the savages drove their knives into his body in many places. John Neal was fatally shot in the left lung in the town, and Waddy Rice seriously in the hand. Four negroes were found on the field and two mortally wounded. Six additional negroes have been found dead about Clinton since. The white men of Clinton were organized at once for self-protection under Colonel Harding, and telegrams sent hence for assistance. Fifteen minutes after the receipt of the first despatch 150 men were ready to march and took a special train, which reached Clinton at seven o'clock.

About ten o'clock more reinforcements came from Jackson. The roads were picketed during the night, but, all danger being apparently over, most of the citizens returned to their homes at Vicksburg, leaving thirty men on guard, under command of Capt. W. H. Andrews. Capt. Andrews returned with the men this morning, and reports all is now quiet at Clinton and Edwards. The train from Jackson on Saturday night, with reinforcements for Clinton, were fired into from the side of the road, and obstructions were also placed on the track.

CLINTON, Miss., Sept. 6.—About forty negroes have been killed and many wounded. The whites hold possession of the town and the negroes have scattered in all directions. The leaders are said to be in Jackson.

The Governor has called on Gen. George, chairman of the Democratic Executive Committee, to assist in restoring order. All is quiet at present—10 P. M.

Another Account.

CHICAGO, Sept. 6.—An *Inter-Ocean* special from Jackson, Miss., says:—

Warren and Hinds counties are in a state of insurrection. The sheriff of Hinds county in his official report to Governor Ames says that he yesterday summoned a posse to quell riotous proceedings.

On arriving at Clinton he found the town quiet, but bands of white men were marauding in the country, shooting peaceable and innocent colored citizens within the town limits even. Detached squads were wandering around driving colored men from their homes. He found it impossible to protect colored men against the parties.

The blacks are unarmed and defenseless. The slaughter of colored men was fearful, and nobody knows where it will end should the Governor not interfere. A gentleman from Raymond says it is believed that over a hundred negroes have been killed within three days. This is merely hearsay, but it is certain fifteen or twenty have perished about Clinton.

White men bearing arms stand at all the depots, and, under pretense of self-defense, shoot down negroes in cold blood. Massacres are reported at several points, but none of these reports are authenticated.

Here is a personal account of the Clinton County Riots by Black Republican Leader Eugene Wellborne:

"They had a barbecue and there were speakers invited. It was a kind of joint discussion. Amos R. Johnston [a Democrat] spoke first. After he got through Capt. H.T. Fisher, who was a Republican, was called upon to speak. There were a couple of young fellows standing in front of me—Sivley and Thompson. These gentlemen were a committee sent from Raymond. In the event that the Republican speakers told anything that they thought was not so, they had a right to contradict them. Captain Fisher had spoke two or three minutes when this Sivley says, "Come down out of there, you god damned radical, you. We don't want to hear any more of your lies."

I spoke to Aleck Wilson who was one of our officers there to keep the peace. We had about thirty men that we got the magistrate to deputize. I saw Wilson and said, "I want you to stand here and prevent anything. I see a difficulty brewing." Thompson had a bottle of whisky in his hand. He was drinking, and every now and then they would holler, "Come down! Stop your damned lying there, and come down."

Wilson went up to Mr. Thompson and said, "Mr. Thompson, we listened very quietly to your speaker and you must not go on in that way." He told him he was an officer and that he would have to arrest him if he did not stop. When Wilson said that, they all got right together around Thompson. He said, "Get away from here." Then Wilson attempted to arrest him and Thompson pulled his pistol out and shot him down. When Wilson fell, every [white] man in the line pulled out their pistols and began to fire on the crowd.

On Sunday—that was on Saturday—they just hunted the whole county clean out. Every man they could see they were shooting at him just the same as birds. I mean colored men, of course. A good many they killed and a good many got away. The men came into Jackson, two or three thousand of them. They were running in all day Sunday, coming in as rapidly as they could. We could hear the firing all the time."[25]

In a telegram, Governor Aldebert Ames pleas for federal government intervention are more closely related to Wellborne's description of the incident. Ames asks for immediate intervention as several riots were breaking out in different counties and armed parties were attempting to take over the government.[26]

CHAPTER 6:
THE SOUTHWEST MISSOURI RIOTS
NEW TOWN, SAME HATE

The tumultuous years between 1894 and 1906 would set the stage for race riots in four Missouri cities. The towns affected were Monett in 1894, Pierce City in 1901, Joplin in 1903 and Springfield in 1906. According to the *Encyclopedia of Race Riots*, "Occurring within a span of 12 years and a radius of eighty miles these riots represent the largest cluster of post- Civil War race riots in American History. The Southwest Missouri riots resulted from a volatile combination of virulent racism, white fears of Black sexual predations, growing African American urban populations, intense labor competition, and, in at least two cases, political rivalry between the two races." In *Sundown Towns*, Loewen explains that some towns drove out Blacks due to jealousy of their all-white neighboring town. He explains that Monett's financial success after forcing Blacks out, possibly led Pierce city to do the same, and Pierce city's expulsion resulted in copycat cases throughout Southwest Missouri and Arkansas.
Southwest Riots

The Southwest riots, each case:

- Originated with a lynching of at least one African American man accused of a violent crime.
- Mobs killed that person then more African Americans.
- Resulted in a large number of Blacks leaving the town and abandoning their property and jobs.
- By fleeing to a nearby city, some of the people would be victimized in other cities. In some cases, Blacks were the victims of riots on three separate cases. Imagine the tenacity that it takes to rebuild after having lost all physical possessions including home, clothing, and furniture and possibly family on three separate occasions.

The first riot, Monett, 1894 [27]

- Population: 3500 residents, 100 Black
- Most worked for the San Francisco Railroad
- Tensions over job competition and 1892 murder of a white man by a black man
- 6/20/1894 at 10 p.m. white and black laborers clashed outside of a saloon. Black man fatally shot Robert Greenwood, a San Francisco Railroad brakeman and grandson of a Bentonville, Arkansas judge.
- Ulysses Hayden was the blamed shooter.
- He was found eight days later in Neosho, MO.
- He claimed to be at the fight, but not the killer.
- His claims were later verified by coroner days later.
- Gang of 50-100 white men, many of them railroad employees, removed the prisoners from law enforcement custody.
- One-mile South of Monett, they hung Hayden from a telegraph pole alongside the railroad tracks.
- Mob ordered all Blacks to leave town or face 'serious reprisals'
- Monett became all-white, a sundown town.

The Second Race Riot, Pierce City, 1901[28]

- Population: 2,151 residents 175 (8%) Black
- The murder of a 19-year-old woman who was found with her throat slashed; and it was believed that the assailant attempted to rape her.
- Witnesses said they saw a Black man near the scene of the crime
- Seventeen-year-old Gene Barrett was arrested; and Will Godley, who had been released recently after serving time for raping an elderly White woman, was arrested.
- On August 19th Godley was lynched. His father was also lynched and burned in his home with another innocent person.
- Barrett was released.
- The riot was larger than Monett as the mob had gathered from nearby towns including Monett.
- They terrorized Blacks throughout the night and the days following. Some were killed, others fled to other towns including Springfield.
- Pierce City would become a sundown town.
- Riots of this nature lead Samuel Clemens (Mark Twain) to ask for Christians Missionaries abroad to come to save the Christians in their home country.
- See more on this riot in the documents that follow these accounts.

The Third Race Riot, Joplin, MO, 1903

- A Black Man was in a shootout with a policeman, Theodore Leslie, who later died.
- On April 16th, 1903, Thomas Gilyard, was accused of the crime.
- Approximately 3,000 members of a mob broke into the jail and lynched him.
- They then turned their fury on other Blacks-injuring people and burning the properties of several Black citizens.
- No one was killed in this riot.
- Most citizens fled to Springfield, MO.

The Fourth Riot, Springfield, MO, 1906

- A White woman, Mina Edwards, claimed that two masked Black men raped her.
- Two Black men, Horace Duncan and Fred Coker were accused of her rape.
- Both men had an alibi as their White employer stated that they were at work at the time of the alleged crime; therefore, they were released.
- When Coker stated that the police had stolen his watch, both men were arrested again.

- A mob broke into the jail and "bludgeoned the men", then dragged their bodies to the town square, lynched them, while men, women and children looked on; they then went back to the jail and took another Black man, Will Allen, lynched him and burned his body.
- People took souvenirs from the crime as they left church on Easter Sunday, April 15th, 1906. Souvenirs included bone fragments and flesh.
- Due to quick action by the Sheriff, the Black community was mostly spared.
- Local shops sold postcards of the lynching.
- Though several were charged with the lynching, no one served time for the murders.
- Edwards recanted her story.
- Black people fled Springfield due to fear of another Race Riot.

Pierce City Riot Documents

Ethnic Heritage: Black

The events of August 18-20, 1901 forever changed the lives of all black citizens of Peirce City. The Peirce City Fire Station, Courthouse and Jail was directly involved in these events, as its fire bell was rung to alert citizens to the murder of Geshel Wild, and later the two black men suspected of the crime were held in and subsequently removed from the jail by an angry mob. Because of the connection between these events and the building, it is significant the area of Ethnic Heritage--Black.

In order to gain insight into how the events of August 18 - 20, 1901 contributed to the overall pattern of events in our history, it may be helpful to note some of the state and national trends prior to this year. In 1883, the United States Supreme Court declared the Civil Rights Act of 1875 unconstitutional. The 1875 law had attempted to ensure blacks access to accomodations such as restaurants and theaters. Following its overturn, southern states passed segregation laws. In 1877 President Rutherford B. Hayes was elected after narrowly defeating Samuel J. Tilden. The election was finally decided by a congressionally appointed commission, and Hayes won only after agreeing to certain concessions to the South, which included the withdrawal of federal troops placed there during Reconstruction.

Missouri's 1875 constitution provided for separate schools for blacks and whites. In 1887, a white teacher in Grundy County, Missouri refused to admit black students to a white school which had previously been open to them, and the parents sued on grounds their 14th Amendment rights had been violated. While this case made its way through the courts, in 1889 the Missouri Legislature passed a law ordering separate schools be established for blacks. In 1890, the Missouri Supreme Court heard the Grundy case, and ruled against the black students. In 1896, the United States Supreme Court established "separate but equal" in Plessy v. Ferguson, making separate but equal accomodations for blacks constitutional. In Missouri, no laws on the subject existed, but custom prevented blacks from joining whites in hotels, theaters, hospitals, and other public places. (While these events in no way justify the events in Peirce City

NPS Form 10-900-a
(8-86)

OMB Approval No. 1024-0018

United States Department of the Interior
National Park Service

National Register of Historic Places
Continuation Sheet

Section _8_   Page _8_

Peirce City Fire Station, Courthouse, and Jail
Lawrence County, Missouri

in 1901, this information is provided to demonstrate how the following events are part of a pattern in our state and national history.)[10]

On August 18, 1901, nineteen year old Geshel Wild was returning to her home two miles west of Peirce City following Sunday school, following the railroad tracks. While only 1/2 mile from the business district, she was attacked, her throat cut and her body thrown into a ditch below a culvert. Her brother, who left church only 15 minutes later, found her and phoned the sheriff from the nearest house. When news reached the city the community's fire bell was rung and great crowds began to gather, "ready to hunt down the inhuman brute." Will Roark stated that "he had seen a negro sitting on the culvert just awhile before the crime was committed, which caused the crowd to suspect who the perpetrator was...."[11]

By Monday, August 19, 1901, "thousands of armed and determined men gathered in Peirce City and the failure to catch the criminal added fuel to the flames and the generally accepted fact that it was a negro that committed the crime aroused the bitterest feeling against that race. This led to the arrest of Will Godley, a notorious negro, and Gene Barrett, on suspicion..."[12]

The two were held in the Peirce City Jail. Monday's headline in the Peirce City Empire read: "FOULLY MURDERED -Geshel Wild's Throat Cut While on her way Home from Church - The Most Atrocious Crime Ever Committed in this Vicinity - The Murderer Supposed to be a Colored Man." The article contained the following suggestion:

> That case of murder which took place just west of the city Sunday evening, and one might say within the glare of the electric lights, was the most awful occurrence our people ever had to contend with, and it is to be sincerely hoped that the guilty wretch may be brought speedily to justice. No such crime should ever be let go unpunished, and every citizen should constitute himself an officer for the time being to help down the murderer. 'Vengeance is mine, sayeth the Lord,' yet in this instance the crime is such that every nick and corner of the city should be thoroughly searched, and when discovered no punishment is too bad.[13]

Around 9:00 p.m. Monday evening, August 19, 1901, the crowd headed for the Peirce City Jail where the two men were being held. Using a sledge hammer, the jail door was broken down, and the two were taken to the Lawrence Hotel downtown where Godley was hung from the awning, then riddled by bullets from the mob. According to a Mount Vernon newspaper,

[10] Lorenzo J. Greene, Gary R. Kremer, and Antonio F. Holland, eds., Missouri's Black Heritage, rev. ed. (Columbia: University of Missouri Press, 1993), p. 104-107.

[11] Peirce City (Missouri) Empire, August 22, 1901.

[12] Mount Vernon (Missouri) Lawrence Chieftain, August 22, 1901, p.1.

[13] Peirce City (Missouri) Empire, August 22, 1901.

NPS Form 10-900-a
(8-86)

OMB Approval No. 1024-0018

United States Department of the Interior
National Park Service

**National Register of Historic Places
Continuation Sheet**

Section _8_   Page _9_

Peirce City Fire Station, Courthouse, and Jail
Lawrence County, Missouri

It is not claimed that Godley killed the young girl, but his reputation was of the worst. He had recently completed a sentence in the penitentiary for rape committed on a white woman 60 years of age, near Peirce City. He was suspected of attempted assault on two young girls.[14]

Following the hanging of Godley, Gene Barrett named two other black men as suspects, and was released. However the mob was not satisfied, and before the night was out French Godley, father of the deceased, and Pete Hampton were shot and burned when the elder Godley's house was burned. Four more houses of black families were burned that night. Tuesday's Peirce City Empire headline read: "HUNG - Will Godley Taken From the City Jail and Hung. Gene Barrett confessed Who Did the Deed."[15] In Mount Vernon, the headline of the Lawrence Chieftain read:

HEINOUS CRIME AT PEIRCE CITY, A Young Lady Assaulted and Brutally Murdered. HER THROAT CUT FROM EAR TO EAR. Mob Law the Result. One Negro, Will Godley, Lynched and Two Others, Pete Hampton and Frank Godley, Riddled With Bullets and Their Bodies Burned in the House Where They Fell. ALL THE NEGROES, 200 IN NUMBER, DRIVEN FROM PEIRCE CITY.[16]

This article describes the riot and subsequent exodus of the black population, in part, as:

The mob was composed of people from Peirce City, Monett and the surrounding country. Every kind of firearm was used by the immense crowd. Hardware stores were broken open and their stocks of guns and pistols seized. The armory of the company of national guards was rifled and every musket taken. The attack on the negroes continued as long as one of the hated race could be found. Most of the colored people ran away from their homes as soon as they saw the bent of the mobs fury. It is about one-fourth of a mile from Peirce City to the woods. Some of the frightened ran to this shelter. Others took the first train and left, never to return. Many did not have time to pack their household goods. Tuesday morning the exodus of the blacks continued and some of the terror stricken people left for Springfield and other places of safety. It is reported that there is not now a colored person left in Peirce City or vicinity.[17]

Wednesday, August 21st, 1901, the Peirce City Empire included a single line stating "Sarah Godley, and the rest of the colored folks took the evening trains yesterday for different points on the Frisco."[18] Eventually a black man named Joe Lark of Peirce City was charged and in November, 1901 was tried for the murder of Geshel Wild, but found not guilty.[19]

---

[14] Mount Vernon (Missouri) Lawrence Chieftain, August 22, 1901. p.1.

[15] Peirce City (Missouri) Empire, August 22, 1901.

[16] Mount Vernon (Missouri) Lawrence Chieftain, August 22, 1901. p.1.

[17] Ibid.

[18] Peirce City (Missouri) Empire, August 22, 1901.

[19] Mount Vernon (Missouri) Lawrence Chieftain, November 28, 1901. p. 1.

NPS Form 10-900-a
(8-86)

OMB Approval No. 1024-0018

United States Department of the Interior
National Park Service

National Register of Historic Places
Continuation Sheet

Section _8_   Page _10_

Peirce City Fire Station, Courthouse, and Jail
Lawrence County, Missouri

Peirce City lost its entire black population during August 18th, 19th and 20th, 1901. This follows the statewide trend, as in 1890, only 47% of Missouri's black population lived in urban areas, but by 1900, this number had increased to 55%. During the 1890's, neglect of blacks by political leaders led many lawless whites to feel they had a license to harass them. This oppression manifested itself in the growing prevalance of lynching throughout Missouri and the nation during the late nineteenth and early twentieth centuries. The late nineteenth century was a violent period in American history. Industrialization shattered the nation's agricultural lifestyle. Labor unrest, financial panics and an increasing number of immigrants challenged whites for jobs, causing them to search for scapegoats. When a scapegoat was found, lynching blacks was a chief form of violence. Around the time of the Peirce City lynching, there were several Pullman railroad strikes reported. In describing Monett's lynching during this period, which occurred in 1894, The Carthage Press reported "the white railroad men were out to drive the Negroes from the city." Clearly from newspaper accounts of the day, there were a considerable number of outsiders in Peirce City, presumably to hunt down Geshel Wild's killer, and railroad workers most likely contributed a good bit to this effort.[20]

The number of lynchings in Missouri reached an all-time high in the 1860's, dropped during the 1870's, but rose again through the 1880's and 1890's, declining somewhat in the early 1900's. While lynching was common in many states, during the late nineteenth century eighty-one people were lynched in Missouri, with fifty-one being black. During the same period, seventy-eight were lynched in Virginia, fifty-three in North Carolina, twenty-four in neighboring Illinois, and twenty-two in Kansas. Mob leaders generally escaped punishment, often with the complicity of legal authorities.[21]

The events in Peirce City during August, 1901 were reported nationally and moved former Missourian Mark Twain to write an essay entitled "The United States of Lyncherdom," which was intended for publication in the North American Review. In his article, Twain mused:

"Why does a crowd . . . stand by, smitten to the heart and miserable, and by ostentatious outward signs pretend to enjoy a lynching? Why does it lift no hand or voice in protest? Only because it would be unpopular to do it, I think; each man is afraid of his neighbor's disapproval, a thing which, to the general run of the race, is more dreaded than wounds and death. When there is to be a lynching the people hitch up and come miles to see it, bringing their wives and children. Really to see it? No--they come only because they are afraid to stay at home, lest it be noticed and offensively commented upon."

Toward the end of the essay, Twain appealed to the missionaries in China to return to the United States to return to where they were equally needed: "O compassionate missionary, leave China! come home and convert these Christians!"[22]

---

[20] Missouri's Black Heritage, Rev. Ed. p. 107-108; and Murray Bishoff, Monett, Missouri, phone interview with Jane Beetem, 12/10/97.

[21] Ibid., p. 108; and Harriet C. Frazier, "The History of Death as Punishment in Missouri," (Chart, Criminal Justice Department, Central Missouri State University, Warrensburg, Missouri   November, 1993).

[22] The Complete Works of Mark Twain: Europe and Elsewhere. (New York: Harper and Brothers, 1923), p. 244-245.

Joplin Riots Documents[29]:

"WHAT IS LEFT IN LIFE FOR A NEGRO IN JOPLIN?"

Sufferer in Last Wednesday's Race Riots, a Peaceful Taxpayer, Whose House Was Burned, Utters Last Appeal.

THE TRIBUNE is in receipt of the following communication from a negro of Joplin, Mo., where last Wednesday evening a mob followed the lynching of a negro by a raid on the colored settlement, driving the black population from the town:

" I, uneducated and ignorant, once a slave, and now a free man, have lived in Joplin for about thirty years. I have been a property owner and taxpayer, and if I refuse to pay my taxes by the law of my country my property would be taken away from me. As I have it in my own name, you can see at once I must be a citizen of the city I call my home, Joplin. I suppose the money I have paid in the way of taxes has gone to school funds to educate people such as came to my house last Wednesday night and broke out my window panes and routed my wife and children and scared them nearly to death. I found them in a box car near the railroad track, crouched in there for a place of safety, and I sit in my house and hear the howling fiends utter oaths that drove me mad: 'Get out, niggers, this is a white man's town.'

" In the air there was an odor of burning kerosene and the angry flames came up from the outer edges of my house. I then thought, it's time for me to vacate. So I turned and said, what next can I do? I have lived and obeyed the people in my community. I have been as meek and humiliating as an old black slave could be to his master, and they still ask more of me. Is it possible I am not fit for h——? Is it that the people of Joplin are so hardened that the divine and forgiven love of God can't move them—the Supreme Being who placed the planets in their sockets and bade them revolve till time shall be no more?

" I regret the necessity that compels me to say that the time is at hand right now. I appeal to ' heaven,' my country first I call, and if no response, and then I guess the last resort for a poor, defenseless, hooted, downtrodden, and unfortunate man who happens to be born with a dark skin is to at last rid myself of this unfair life, and on the other side of the border lands of eternity there will be equal rights and special privileges to no one.

" Now, would I say again, I would say, O Lord, if there is any, have mercy on my soul, if a black man who lives in Joplin has any."

Springfield, MO Riots Documents

Horace Duncan

CHAPTER 7:
EAST SAINT LOUIS RIOTS:
AN AMERICAN POGROM

1917 marked a tumultuous year in race relations in America. In 1915, the movie *Birth of a Nation,* which depicted Black men as savages whose insatiable desire to rape white women could only be quelled by the Ku Klux Klan was screened in the White House. The screening of this movie by President Woodrow Wilson gave the movie greater credibility and led to a rise in Klan membership.

This resurgence of hate, coupled with Wilson's 1916 run for president wherein the Democratic party's cries of Colonization: the idea of Blacks being brought from the South to bolster the Republican Party; and the competition between Whites and Blacks for low-paying jobs in the factories, led to one of the worst race riots in history. In 1917, riots occurred in both Houston and Chester, Pennsylvania, but the riot which Professor Charles Lumpkin referred to as an American Pogrom, or an ethnic cleansing was the East St. louis Race Riot, which began on July 2, 1917. *The Crisis* newspaper lists the loss of life of Blacks at 126, but the actual number is still unknown. Many victims were burned or thrown into the river, and their bodies were never recovered. Thousands of Blacks fled East St. Louis and never returned. Some moved just across the river to St. Louis where they had received refuge after the riots.

The NAACP, which was founded as a result of a race riot in Springfield, Illinois in 1908, sent W. E.B. Dubois (himself a victim of a race riot in Atlanta in 1906) and Martha Gruening to East St. Louis to investigate. The Negro Fellowship League sent antilynching activist Ida B. Wells to East St. Louis to investigate. Each took first person accounts of the atrocities that occurred in the city.

First Person Accounts Taken by Ida B. Wells -Barnett, and reported in *The East St. Louis Massacre: The Greatest Outrage of the Century:*[30]

Mrs. Dolly Bruton, another widow, came to East St. Louis from Mississippi, December 8th, 1915. She had left two trunks full of clothes at 513 Collinsville Ave., because she had been told that the worst of the riot was over and it was alright for her to stay in East St. Louis. But on this very morning of July 5th, a soldier had come into this house and began to search for weapons. He found nobody there but Mrs. Mary Howard and three other women, one of whom was ill. When he could find no gun, he arrested every one of those women and brought them to the City Hall. They were bare headed and in the soiled clothing they had worn about their work at home. Mrs. Howard said, that she had lived in East St. Louis eighteen years. Her husband, Douglass Howard, was a grader, making $19.35 a week. They owned four houses and lots in East St. Louis. She had seen a good part of the rioting Tuesday, but had not been disturbed herself. She thought it was because her house was right between the homes and stores of some of the white people. Just as she had thought the whole thing was over, it both frightened and humiliated her to be subjected to this outrage at the hands of the soldiers at the time that General Dickson was in charge of the situation and everybody had been assured that the danger was over.

That was the last straw with her. She too wanted protection to go out to her home and get her things so she could leave town. She said that during the riot a young fellow whom she had sent to the grocery to get a chicken, was knocked off his wheel by the mob. Then the mob took his wheel and struck him on the side of his head with a brick and knocked a hole in it. His name was Jimmie Eckford, eighteen years old and roomed at her house. He ran into the nearest yard which happened to be that of white people. When the mob said they would burn this house down if they didn't make

Eckford come out, the tenants picked him up and threw him out in the street to the mob where he was kicked and stamped on and beaten till they knocked his teeth from his head and killed him.

The street cars ran right along in front of her house, and she saw white women stop the street cars and pull colored women off and beat them. One woman's clothes they tore off entirely, and then took off their shoes and beat her over the face and head with their shoe heels. Another woman who got away, ran down the street with every stitch of clothes torn off her back, leaving her with only her shoes and stockings on. Mrs. Howard saw two men beaten to death. She had escaped all excepting having rocks thrown at the house, until this soldier humiliated her by coming into her house and arresting her and the other women there, because they couldn't find any guns concealed. This happened on the morning of the 5th.

Clarrissa Lockett's Account.

Mrs. Lockett lived in the house with her brother where she had been ever since both he and she came from Mississippi. Her brother worked nights, so that all during the rioting Monday night she was alone. They didn't get to set fire to her house that night, but she sat up all night long waiting. She was unwilling to leave her household goods until she had to. She went to work at the packing house Tuesday morning early, but quit at 9 A. M. The soldiers who were guarding the plant took her and the other colored women home. Tuesday night the mob came to her number, 48 Third street, rear. After they had set fire to it and run her out, she ran into a Polish saloon not far away and the saloonkeeper and his wife agreed to let her stay there that night, although they knew the risk they ran in so doing. They told her to crouch down behind the piano and to stay there quietly all night. This she did, glad of the chance. She had been able only to bring her dog and her gun when she ran out of her home. After the saloonkeeper and his wife had gone upstairs to bed about 1 o'clock in the morning, the barkeeper and a man friend of his came back behind the piano and attempted to assault her. She drew her pistol and drove them off. When they found she had a gun, they left her in peace until morning. Early Wednesday morning, the day of our national independence, she found a man who hauled her trunk containing her own and her brother's clothes over into St. Louis, Missouri. She left two rooms filled with new furniture. She saw soldiers take guns and knives from colored men, and then the mob would set on them and beat or murder them.

When I saw her at St. Louis, Missouri, she had not yet recovered from the shock. Her brother had come straight out of the packing plant for which he was working and went straight to the train in his working clothes and went to Meridian, Mississippi, his former home. She was very anxious until she got a card letting her know where he was.

Mrs. Josie Nixon whose husband Samuel and daughter Pearl had lived in their home in East St. Louis thirteen years. The family is well known and respected. Her husband is a carpenter and contractor. Her daughter has finished her third year in high school and she had been working at Swift's for nine months. The mob did not harm her or her husband at her home, but the excitement was so great, she was still suffering from the nervous strain. She said, that although they knew about the excitement and the burning of homes the night before, that on Tuesday morning at 5:30 o'clock, she and a man and his wife started to work that early, thinking that they would avoid the mob. They met a young fellow about nineteen or twenty years old, walking down the street with a soldier who had a gun. "This young fellow held up the man who was with us and searched him, and asked him where he was going, told him not to come back this way and that he had better be out of town by night, if not, he, the white man, would get him if he had to set his house afire." All this while the soldier in Uncle Sam's uniform was standing by with his gun, and he said too, "Yes, you'd better get out of town."

She went back home and she and her daughter sat there nearly all day, fearing attack at any moment. She had not seen or heard of her husband since the day before. Fearing that some harm had come to him and having not a nickel in the house, she borrowed carfare from the druggist across from her home and leaving her comfortable home, went over into St. Louis. Late that evening, her husband came home and finding them gone, he hunted all over town, but nobody could tell him about her. He stayed in his house Tuesday night and saw two sons of a white neighbor of his set fire to his house. He ran and put out the fire himself, thus saving his home.

Mrs. Nixon saw a woman whose tongue was shot off when she was shot through the mouth, being taken to the hospital. She begged the police to go back for her son who was in the house. They found him lying behind a trunk shot dead. She said that woman was still in the hospital.
The mob went into one house near her, beat the man who was at home until he fainted. He begged them to spare him on account of his wife and new born baby who were in a rear room. When he revived he found both wife and baby dead in the bed where the mob had killed them.

They only left him because they thought he was dead. She knew of another case, whereas the mother came rushing out of the flames of her home, with her baby in her arms, the baby was shot through the head and thrown back into the fire. Many children were killed in this way.
Mrs. Nixon had three gardens planted besides having this nice home and she felt that the mob would not harm her because she was so well and she felt that the mob would not harm her because she was so well known. After they told her that the excitement was all over, she went back to East St. Louis on Thursday morning and went again to her job. While she was at work that morning, a white man standing talking to a bunch of other men said, loud enough for her to hear, "If I have to leave here and give my place to a nigger, I'll certainly kill me a lot of niggers before I go, to pay for it." All the white men in the crowd turned and glared at her in so menacing a fashion that she lost her nerve completely, threw up her job, went back to St. Louis, Missouri, and had rented her a house for the purpose of living over there.

Many of the women complained that the soldiers would not let them go into their homes except to get a few clothes. These and many other such stories all testify to the same thing, that the soldiers did not offer any protection to colored people, but did search them and take their fire arms from them and then stand aside and left them helpless before the mob.

Wells report also includes a newspaper report:

From the St. Louis Post Dispatch, July 3rd, 1917.

By Carlos F. Hurd, Staff Reporter.

For an hour and a half last evening I saw the massacre of helpless Negroes at Broadway and Fourth street, in downtown East St. Louis, where a black skin was a death warrant.

I have read of St. Bartholomew's night. I have heard stories of the latter-day crimes of the Turks in Armenia, and I have learned to loathe the German army for its barbarity in Belgium. But I do not believe that Moslem fanatism or Prussian frightfulness could perpetrate murders of more deliberate brutality than those which I saw committed in daylight by citizens of the State of Abraham Lincoln.

I saw man after man, with hands raised, pleading for his life, surrounded by groups of men - men who had never seen him before and knew nothing about him except that he was black - and saw them administer the historic sentence of intolerance, death by stoning. I saw one of these men, almost dead from a savage shower of stones, hanged with a clothes line, and when it broke, hanged with a rope which held. Within a few spaces of the pole from which he was suspended, four other Negroes lay dead or dying, another had been removed, dead, a short time before. I saw the pockets of two of these Negroes searched, without the finding of any weapon.

I saw one of these men, covered with blood and half conscious, raise himself on his elbow, and look feebly about, when a young man, standing directly behind, lifted a flat stone and hurled it directly upon his neck. This young man was much better dressed than most of the others. He walked away unmolested.

I saw Negro women begging for mercy and pleading that they had harmed no one, set upon by white women of the baser sort, who laughed and answered the course sallies of men as they beat the Negresses' faces and breasts with fists, stones and sticks. I saw one of these furies fling herself at a militiaman who was trying to protect a Negress, and wrestle with him for his bayonetted gun, while other women attacked the refugee.

What I saw, in the 90 minutes between 6:30 P. M. and the lurid coming of darkness, was but one local scene of the drama of death. I am satisfied that, in spirit and method, it typified the whole. And I cannot somehow speak of what I saw as mob violence. It was not my idea of a mob.

A mob is passionate, a mob follows one man or a few men blindly; a mob sometimes take chances. The East St. Louis affair, as I saw it, was a man hunt, conducted on a sporting basis, though with anything but the fair play which is the principle of the sport. The East St. Louis men took no chances, except the chance from stray shots, which every spectator of their acts took. They went in small groups, there was little leadership, and there was a horribly cool deliberateness and a spirit of fun about it. I cannot allow even the doubtful excuse of drink. No man whom I saw showed the effect of liquor. It was no crowd of hot-headed youths. Young men were in the greater number, but there were the middle-aged, no less active in the task of destroying the life of every discoverable black man. It was a shirtsleeve gathering, and the men were mostly workingmen, except for some who had the aspect of mere loafers. I have mentioned the peculiarly brutal crime committed by the only man there who had the appearance of being a business or professional man of any standing.

I would be more pessimistic about my fellow-Americans than I am today, if I could not say that there were other workingmen who protested against the senseless slaughter. I would be ashamed of myself if I could not say that I forgot my place as a professional observer and joined in such protests. But I do not think any verbal objection had the slightest effect. Only a volley of lead would have stopped those murderers.

"Get a nigger," was the slogan, and it was varied by the recurrent cry, "Get another!" It was like nothing so much as the holiday crowd, with thumbs turned down, in the Roman Coliseum, except that here the shouters were their own gladiators, and their own wild beasts.
When I got off a State street car on Broadway at 6:30, a fire apparatus was on its way to the blaze in the rear of Fourth street, south from Broadway. A moment's survey showed why this fire had been set, and what it was meant to accomplish.

The sheds in the rear of Negroes' houses, which were themselves in the rear of the main buildings on Fourth street, had been ignited to drive out the Negro occupants of the houses. And the slayers were waiting for them to come out.

It was stay in and be roasted, or come out and be slaughtered. A moment before I arrived, one Negro had taken the desperate chance of coming out, and the rattle of revolver shots, which I heard as I approached the corner, was followed by the cry, "They've got him!"

And they had. He lay on the pavement, a bullet wound in his head and his skull bare in two places. At every movement of pain which showed that life still remained, there came a terrific kick in the jaw or the nose, or a crashing stone, from some of the men who stood over him.
At the corner, a few steps away, were a Sergeant and several guardsmen. The Sergeant approached the ring of men around the prostrate Negro.

"This man is done for," he said. "You'd better get him away from here. No one made a move to lift the blood-covered form, and the Sergeant walked away, remarking, when I questioned him about an ambulance, that the ambulances had quit coming. However, an undertaker's ambulance did come 15 minutes later, and took away the lifeless Negro, who had in the meantime been further kicked and stoned.

By that time, the fire in the rear of the Negro houses had grown hotter, and men were standing in all the narrow spaces through which the Negroes might come to the street. There was talk of a Negro, in one of the houses, who had a Winchester, and the opinion was expressed that he had no ammunition left, but no one went too near, and the fire was depended on to drive him out. The firemen were at work on Broadway, some distance east, but the flames immediately in the rear of the Negro houses burned without hindrance.

A half-block to the south, there was a hue and a cry at a railroad crossing, and a fusillade of shots were heard. More militiamen than I have seen elsewhere, up to that time, were standing on a platform and near a string of freight cars, trying to keep back men who had started to pursue

Negroes along the track.

As I turned back toward Broadway, there was a shout at the alley, and a Negro ran out, apparently hoping to find protection. He paid no attention to missiles thrown from behind, none of which had hurt him much, but he was stopped in the middle of the street by a smashing blow in the jaw, struck by a man he had not seen.

"Don't do that," he appealed. "I haven't hurt nobody." The answer was a blow from one side, a piece of curbstone from the other side, and a push which sent him on the brick pavement. He did not rise again, and the battering and the kicking of his skull continued until he lay still, his blood flowing half way across the street. Before he had been booted to the opposite curb, another Negro appeared, and the same deeds were repeated. I did not see any revolver shots fired at these men. Bullets and ammunition were used for use at longer range. It was the last Negro I have mentioned who was apparently finished by the stone hurled upon his neck by the noticeably well-dressed young man.

The butchering of the fire-trapped Negroes went on so rapidly that, when I walked back to the alley a few minutes later, one was lying dead in the alley on the west side of Fourth street and another on the east side.

And now women began to appear. One frightened black girl probably 20 years old, got as far as Broadway with not worse treatment than jeers and thrusts. At Broadway, in view of militiamen, the white women, several of whom had been watching the massacre of the Negro men, pounced on the Negress. I do not wish to be understood as saying that these women were representatives of the womanhood of East St. Louis. Their faces showed, all too plainly, exactly who and what they were. But they were the heroines of the moment with that gathering of men, and when one man, sick of the brutality he had seen, seized one of the women by the arm to stop an impending blow, he was hustled away with fists under his nose, and with more show of actual anger than had been bestowed upon any of the Negroes. He was a stocky, nervy chap, and he stood his ground until a diversion elsewhere drew the menacing ring of men away.

"Let the girls have her," was the shout as the women attacked the young Negress. The victim's cry, "Please, please, I ain't done nothing," was stopped by a blow in the mouth with a broomstick, which one of the women swung like a baseball bat. Another women seized the Negress' hands and the blow was repeated as she struggled helplessly. Finger nails clawed her hair, and the sleeves were torn from her waist, when some of the men called, "Now let her see how fast she can run." The women did not readily leave off beating

her, but they stopped short of murder, and the crying, hysterical girl ran down the street. An older Negress a few moments later came along with two or three militiamen, and the same women made for her. When one of the soldiers held his gun as a barrier, the woman with the broomstick seized it with both hands and struggled to wrest it from him, while the others, striking at the Negress, in spite of the other militiamen, frightened her thoroughly and hurt her somewhat.

From Negress baiting, the well-pleased procession turned to see a lynching. A Negro had his head laid open by a great stone-cut, had been dragged to the mouth of the alley on 4th street and a small rope was being tied about his neck. It broke when it was pulled over a projecting cable, letting the Negro fall. A stouter rope was secured.

Right here I saw the most sickening sight of the evening. To put the rope around the Negro's neck, one of the lynchers stuck his fingers inside the gaping scalp and lifted the Negro's head by it, literally bathing his hand in the man's blood. "Get hold and pull for East St. Louis," called a man with a black coat and a new straw hat on as he seized the other end of the rope, and helped lift the body seven feet from the ground, and left hanging there.

A mob of white men formed and burned all the Negro houses on Bond Avenue between Tenth and Twelfth Streets, 43 houses being destroyed.

In the fire zone at Sixth and Broadway, two Negroes are reported to have burned to death. At Fifth and Railroad, another death by fire was reported. One of the mid-afternoon killings was at 4 o'clock, at Broadway and Main Street. A Negro was shot down. One of those firing on him being a boy in short trousers. The driver of the first ambulance that came was not permitted to remove this body, and it lay for an hour beside the street car tracks seen by the passengers in every passing car.

At 9:30 this morning a Negro, still living, but in a critical condition, was found in a sewer manhole at Sixth Street and Broadway. He was beaten by the mob with paving bricks 13 hours before and thrown in.

The 2-year old Negro child who was killed was the daughter of William Forest of 1118 Division Ave. A bullet fired into the house entered the body near the heart.

City Attorney Fekete is credited with having saved the life of a young Negro who was running from a crowd which had fired a number of shots at him while the Negro was plainly visible in the glare of the burning buildings. Fekete placed the Negro in his own automobile, and after arguing for several minutes with the group of men succeeded getting away with the rescued man.

James Taylor's Account

The mob started at 2:05 A. M. At 4:15 they hanged two Negroes who were coming from work, to a telegraph pole and shot them to pieces. Saw them rush to cars and pull women off and beat them to death, and before they were quite dead, stalwart men jumped on their stomachs and finished them by tramping them to death. This was at the corner of Broadway and Collinsville. The cars were crowded and moving, yet they jumped on and pulled them off. Others they stuck to death with hat pins, sometimes picking out their eyes with them before they were quite dead.

An old woman between 70 and 80 years old, who had returned to her house to get some things, was struck almost to death by women, then men stamped her to death.

A colored store keeper at 8th and Broadway with his family was shot and wounded. The store was set on fire and they burned to death.

George Launders and Robert Mosely were burned to death at the Library Flats at 8th and Walnut.

Rev. James Taylor's wife fled to the Broadway theatre with her five children, but left there in safety before it was burned. She said when she left there were about twenty-five white women in the basement of the theatre where they had sought safety.

There were 10 or 12 men with Rev. Taylor when he made a dash for safety, several of them armed. Doesn't know if any of them escaped.

He saw a soldier hand his gun to one of the mob.

Had narrow escape as there were men in autos and on motor cycles who shot into the grass and bushes everywhere they thought anyone might be hiding. Came across woman also hiding, who were frightened almost to death. Swam the Cahokia River with her.

Men had fingers cut off by mob, then heads split open with axes.

Colored people acted bravely in spite of handicaps.

Mr. Taylor said, he was searched 29 times for fire arms.

Colored men were frequently beaten while enroute to and from packing houses, with no protest from companies or police.

"The first and last shot fired at me was by a soldier in uniform."

Will Morgan, employed at the B. & O. roundhouse, saw the mob make the Negroes swim into the Cahokia River, then shoot them, one being killed instantly. The other managed to struggle back to shore, only to be stoned to death by children.

Soldiers surrounded the home of William Bass. One of them went inside and drove husband, wife and 9 children out. Asked Mr. Bass if they had any guns. He replied, that he had one, but that it was no good. "Have you any money?" he asked. Receiving a negative reply, he cursed and walked out.

Mr. Buchanan's Story:

Mr. Buchanan says: He did not see a single soldier, excepting Col. Tripp, do anything to protect the Negroes. He formed a hollow square and made the first arrest of about 200, composed of women and men. He also took a rope from the neck of a Negro whom the mob had attempted to hang. Mr. Buchanan saw them beat men down with revolvers and clubs; white men knock Negro women down and then the white women would finish by beating them to death or nearly so.

Every Negro man that he saw get out of Black Valley alive, the soldiers would march them to the police station, badly beaten though they were, and scarcely able to walk, with their hands raised in front of them and afraid to turn their heads. The mob threw bricks at their heads and bodies, because the soldiers had their bayonets pointed at either side of them. They did the women the same way, excepting their hands were not raised in front of them. They were dodging around the soldiers to keep the mob from hitting them with bricks, stones and sticks. Their clothing was badly torn.

A man who worked for the Hill Thomas Lime & Cement Co. on 6th and Walnut streets, after the building had caught fire and was surrounded by the mob, called the manager up and said, "The whole place is on fire, and if I stay it is death and if I leave it is death. I am going to stay. Good-bye."

Mr. Buchanan escaped death by hiding in the Southern Illinois National Bank where he was employed as a messenger. C. Reeb, president of the bank, procured an automobile and took Mr. Buchanan and family, escorted by soldiers, to St. Louis. Mr. Buchanan still works at the bank but is undecided about the future. He said, they were almost sure one of the employees of the bank, a clerk, was one of the rioters and that the president was doing all in his power to obtain the facts about it, and had told him, if he was guilty he would see to it that his punishment fit the crime.

Report from the Crisis Newspaper Article: *The Massacre of East St. Louis*[31]

This is the testimony of Mary Edwards. She is twenty-three years old, directress of a cafeteria at Lincoln School at fifty dollars a month, has lived in East St. Louis for sixteen years:

Knew at ten o'clock in the morning that white and colored had been fighting, but did not know seriousness of fight until five o'clock in evening when riot started at Broadway and Fourth Street. Heard shoot-ing and yelling, saw mob pull women off street cars and beat them, but did not think rioters would come up to Eighth Street. Fires had started and were as far as Fifth Street and Broadway and swept through Fourth St., to Fifth and on to Eighth. The shooting was so violent that they were afraid to leave home. By this time rioters were on Eighth Street, shooting through homes and setting fire to them. Daughter and father were in house dodging bullets which were coming- thick. Building at corner of Eighth and Walnut was occupied by whites. Some of mob yelled, "Save it. Whites live there." Some of the rioters went to Eighth and Broadway and set fire to colored grocery store and colored barber shop. Man in barber shop escaped but the man and wife in store were burned up. By that time Opera House was on fire and flats on side and back of it. East end of Library Flat caught and heat was so great that father and daughter tried to escape through alley and up street to Broadway, but encountered mob at Broadway. Soldiers were in line-up on north side of street and offered no assistance. Ran across street to Westbrook's home with bullets flying all around them and rioters shouting, "Kill him, kill him." Here, daughter lost track of father. She beat on back door of Westbrook's home but no response, ran across alley to Division Avenue, ran on white lady's porch, but the lady would not let her in. Men were shooting at her for all they were worth, but she succeeded in dodging bullets.

Ran across field and got in house and crawled under bed. Mob following right behind her, but lost sight of which house

she went in and set fire to each encl of flat. Rather than be burned to death she ran out and mob began shooting at her again. Just at that time a man ran out of the house, and mob let girl alone and started at him. She fell in weeds and lay very quiet. Could see them beating man. About one hour afterwards she heard someone

ay, "Any niggers in here?" She kept very quiet thinking them rioters. One said, "No one does answer. Come on, boys, let's go m after them." She then raised up not knowing they were soldiers and pleaded for her life. They picked her up and took her over the same ground she had run from the mob: put her in a machine and took her to City Hall. When she came to her-self she was in the doctor's office surround-ed by friends and her sister. Josephine, who had escaped with the Westbrooks. It was about one o'clock when she reached the City Hall.

Mr. Edwards succeeded in getting away from mob, hid under a white man's porch until three o'clock in the morning crawled from under there and went uncle;. side walk on Broadway and stayed there till five o'clock. (In East St. Louis, Ill., the streets are higher than the houses). He got out from under the walk and walked over where his home was still burning and stayed there till five-thirty. Started out to find girls, saw a policeman who told him he would probably find them at City Hall.

On the way to City Hall, he met two policemen with two colored men. One man asked him

if he would send a message to his wife. Mr. Edwards said he could not do so. Po-liceman then arrested him charging him with being one of the rioters. He was locked up in jail and did not get out until twelve o'clock, when he was carried before Justice of Peace for trial. They found him guilty and set his trial for nine o'clock Wednes-day morning and told him he would have to give bond for three hundred dollars. They would not let him have an attorney nor would they let him send for any one. He then asked the Judge to let him make a statement to the court. That was granted. He got up and told of his experience from five o'clock Monday evening until he was arrested at 5: 45 Tuesday morning. After hearing his story the Judge dismissed him.

Daisy and Cora Westbrook are mentioned in Mary Edwards account. Both women were prominent, Black citizens of East St. Louis, and school teachers. Both women offered testimony that the Leroy Bundy, the Black person who was charged with starting the riot was with them, driving in Forest Park at the time of the shooting of the two police officers that sparked the riot.[32]

Daisy Westbrook wrote a letter to her friend Louise. This personal account to a friend offers a rare look into the horrors of race riots. Its personal nature is devoid of the formality that

can be seen in interviews and testimony and offers a more private look into the horrors of the riot.

July 19, 1917 - Dearest Louise: Was very glad to hear from you. Your letter was forwarded from what used to be my house. Louise, it was awful. I hardly know where to begin telling you about it. First I will say we lost everything but what we had on and that was very little - bungalow aprons, no hats, and sister did not have on any shoes. It started early in the afternoon. We kept receiving calls over the 'phone to pack our trunks and leave, because it was going to be awful at night. We did not heed the calls, but sent grandma and the baby on to St. Louis, and said we would "stick" no matter what happened. At first, when the fire started, we stood on Broadway and watched it. As they neared our house we went in and went to the basement. It was too late to run then. They shot and yelled some things awful, finally they reached out house. At first, they did not bother us (we watched from the basement window), they remarked that "white people live in that house, that is not a nigger house." Later, someone must have tipped them that it was a "nigger" house, because, after leaving us for about 20 min, they returned and started shooting in the house throwing bricks and yelling like mad, "kill the niggers," burn that house. It seemed the whole house was falling in on us. Then someone said, they must not be there, if they are they are certainly dead. Then someone shouted, "They are in the basement. Surround them and burn it down." Then they ran down our steps. Only prayer saved us, we were under tubs and anything we could find praying and keeping as quite as possible, because if they had seen one face, we would have been shot or burned to death. When they were about to surround the house and burn it, we heard an awful noise and thought probably they were dynamiting the house. (The Broadway Theatre fell in, we learned later). Sister tipped to the door to see if the house was on fire. She saw the reflection of a soldier on the front door - pulled it open quickly and called for help. All of us ran out then, and was taken to the city hall for the night - (just as we were). The next morning, we learned our house was not burned, so we tried to get protection to go and get clothes, and have the rest of the things put in storage. We could not, but were sent on to St. Louis.

Had to walk across the bridge with a line of soldiers on each side, in the hot sun, no hats and scarcely no clothing. When we reached St. Louis; we tried to get someone to go to our house and get things out, but were not successful. On Tuesday evening at 6 o'clock our house was burned with two soldiers on guard. So the papers stated. We were told that they looted the house before burning it.

We are in St. Louis now trying to start all over again. Louise it is so hard to think we had just gotten to the place where we could take care of our mother and grandmother well, and to think, all was destroyed in one night. We had just bought some new furniture and I was preparing to go away, and had bought some beautiful dresses. Most of my jewelry was lost also. I had on three rings, my watch bracelet and Lavaliere - Everything else was lost, 91 rings, a watch, bracelet, brooch, locket, and some more things. I miss my piano more than anything else. The people here are very nice to us. Several of our friends have brought us clothing, bed clothes, etc. Tell me how you got in the Gov. Printing Office. Do you take an examination, if so, what does it consist of? I might take it. I have had a good position in E. St. L. , but don't know whether there will be enough children to teach there this fall or not. People are moving out so fast. The papers did not describe all the horrors. It was awful. People were being shot down and thrown back into fire if they tried to escape. Some were shot and then burned; others were dragged around with ropes about their necks, one man was hung to a telegraph post. We saw two men shot down. One was almost in front of our house. One man and his wife, a storekeeper, were burned alive, a cross in front of our house. I must close now it makes me blue to talk about it. Write again. Tell Miss Black I received her card. Will you tell Florence & Mrs. Bowie, I haven't their address? Will expect to hear from you real soon. All send love.

Lovingly, Daisy

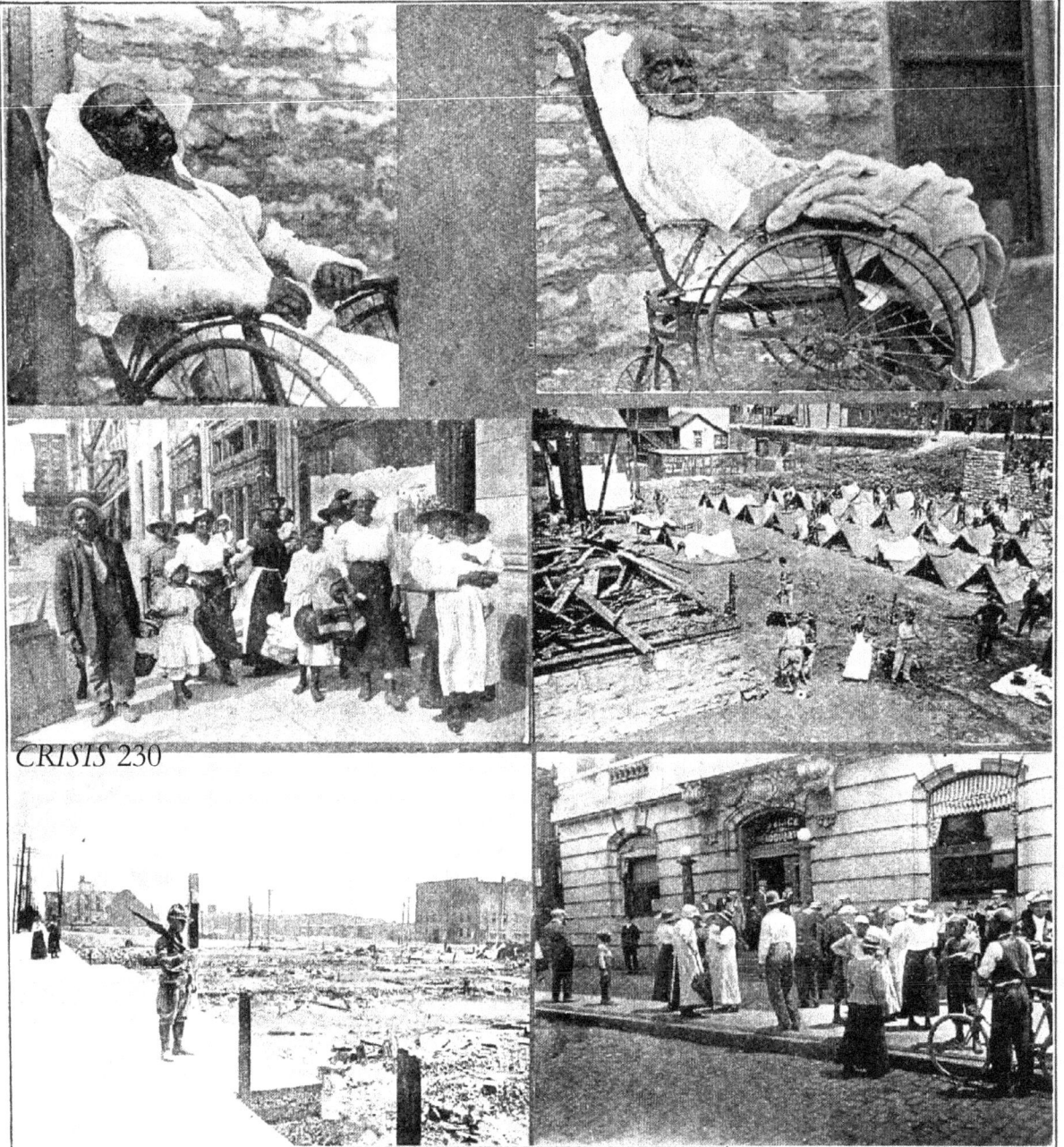

CRISIS 230

FRANK SMITH, BURNED.
THE REFUGEES.
AFTER THE FIRE.

AMOS DAVIS, AGE 84, SHOT.
CAMP OF TROOP D, 1ST ILL. CAVALRY FROM SPRINGFIELD.
POLICE HEADQUARTERS, ST. LOUIS, MO.

CHAPTER 8: RACE RIOTS THROUGHOUT THE COUNTRY: RED SUMMER, 1919

In 1919, more than 25 race riots occurred throughout the country. The actual number is unclear. Many scholars have the number at 25. In *Dusk of Dawn,* W.E.B. Dubois puts the number at 26. Others have mentioned numbers as high as 30. The numbers may be hard to define because of the still unclear definition of a Race Riot. Could the destruction of a courthouse in Omaha, in a successful attempt to force law enforcement to turnover a Black man and allow the mob to lynch him be considered a 'riot', a lynching, or both?[33] The definitions for riots were precarious at best, since it was not uncommon for several Blacks to be killed by a mob of whites. Though the number of riots is unclear, one thing is certain,1919 was one of the deadliest summers in American History. James Weldon Johnson, of the NAACP named it the Red Summer to signify the blood that ran through the streets of America. Though many scholars have proposed several possible reasons for the widespread mob violence, which spread throughout the country, such as The Great Migration, Black Soldiers coming back from the war, the Communist Scare, the mentality of "The New Negro", etc., the circumstances that precipitated many of the riots in 1919 were identical to the circumstances mentioned in chapter one of this text that led to the 1824 Race Riots.

Prior to the riots:
- False accusations of Blacks being immoral or violent
- Blacks in the area attempting to assert their rights.
- Previous violence towards Blacks in the area.
- Failure by law enforcement or political figures to punish those accused of assaults against Blacks, establishing a pattern that violence against Black citizens would be tolerated

A letter written to the *Chicago Tribune,* by antilynching crusader Ida B. Wells-Barnett, wherein she recounts incidents of bombings of Black's homes, attacks on children, and a lack of public outcry and legal intervention prior to the Race Riots in Chicago, mirrors circumstances prior to the Race Riot in Rhode Island almost a century before the riot in 1919. Moreover, in 1824 none of the proposed reasons for the 1919 Race Riots existed.

In the letter, Wells-Barnett foretells that if these circumstances persist, a Race Riot akin to the one in East St. Louis would occur. The following letter was written less than one month prior to the Chicago Race Riots which began on July 27th and ended on August 3rd.

THE RACE PROBLEM IN CHICAGO.

Chicago, June 30.—[Editor of The Tribune.]—With one Negro dead as the result of a race riot last week, another one very badly injured in the county hospital; with a half dozen attacks upon Negro children, and one on the Thirty-fifth street car Tuesday, in which four white men beat one colored man, it looks very much like Chicago is trying to rival the south in its race hatred against the Negro. Especially does this seem so when we consider the bombing Negro homes and the indifference of the public to these outrages.

It is just such a situation as this which led up to the East St. Louis riot two years ago. There had been a half dozen outbreaks against the colored people by whites. Two different committees waited upon Gov. Lowden and asked him to investigate the outrages against Negroes before the riot took place. Nobody paid any attention.

Will the legal, moral, and civic forces of this town stand idly by and take no notice here of these preliminary outbreaks? Will no action be taken to prevent these law breakers until further disaster has occurred?

An ounce of prevention beats a pound of cure. And in all earnestness I implore Chicago to set the wheels of justice in motion before it is too late, and Chicago be disgraced by some of the bloody outrages that have disgraced East St. Louis. IDA B. WELLS-BARNETT.

As stated in chapter one, failure to quell mobs and adequately prosecute white rioters, according to *Sundown Towns: A Hidden Dimension of American Racism*[34], would embolden rioters and lead to repeated riots. This was also the case in 1919. The only difference was that in 1919, instead of several months or years between the Race Riots, the Riots happened in rapid succession. The failure to stop mob attacks was evident as many riots lasted for days prior to a city or state official calling for federal troops to intervene. The longest Race Riot, seven days, occurred in Chicago between July 27th and August 3rd. The Riot in Washington D.C., our nation's capital, lasted for six days. Moreover, the deadliest Race Riot in 1919 was the Elaine, Arkansas Race Riot, which claimed the lives of between 100 and 200 Black people. The final number is unknown. In each case, days of violence lapsed prior to federal troops being called-in. In some cases, such as in Charleston, federal troops were the rioters. By the end of 1919, President Wilson, who had previously shown the *Birth of a Nation* in the White House, had ran a racially divisive campaign, and was a devout segregationist wanted an end to violence as he attempted to uphold the view of America as the purveyor of justice. Furthermore, city and state leaders, were concerned with how mob attacks may affect their business prospects. Therefore, immediate governmental intervention in mob attacks became the norm.

Charleston
May 10th, 1919 was the first day of the Race Riot in Charleston. The Navy concluded that the most likely cause of this incident was a random encounter between Blacks and Whites on the sidewalk. Ironically, this is the same stated reason for the 1824 Rhode Island Race Riot. Moreover, unlike other cities, the Black population in Charleston, according to the Charleston County Public Library Page,[35] was lower than prior to the Great Migration.

Elaine and Omaha as explained in *The Crisis* newspaper:
"The Real Causes of Two Race Riots"[36]

ARKANSAS
THE Thirteenth Amendment to the Constitution of the United States has never been enforced thoroughly. This means that involuntary servitude is still wide spread in the southern United States. There are even vestiges of the slave trade in the convict lease system and the arrangements for trading tenants. On the whole, however, the slavery that remains is a wide spread system of debt peonage and a map of the farms operated by colored tenants shows approximately the extent of this peonage.

The Arkansas riot originated in the attempt of the black peons of the so-called Delta region, (that is the lowlands between Tennessee, Mississippi, Arkansas, and Louisiana) to raise their income. The center, Phillips County, Ark., has 692,000 square miles of land and its chief city is Helena. In 1910 there were 33,535 inhabitants in the country, of whom 26,354 or 78.6% were Negroes. The county is predominately a farming community with $9,000,000 worth of farm property, and two- thirds of the value of all the crops is represented by the cotton crop. Of the 9,835 males of voting age, 7,479 are Negroes, and of these 5,510 could read and write; nevertheless, all the political power is in the hands of the 4,000 white voters, Negroes having no representation even on juries.

The Negroes are the cotton raisers. Of the 30,000 bales of cotton raised in 1909, they raised 25,000. Most of the Negro farmers are tenants. In the whole county there were, in 1910, 587 colored owners and 1,598 colored tenants. These tenants farmed 81,000 acres of land and raised 21,000 bales of cotton. For the most part the method of dealing with these tenants is described by a local reporter, as follows:

All the white plantation owners had a system whereby the Negro tenants and sharecroppers are "furnished" their supplies. They get all their food, clothing, and supplies from the "commissary" or store operated by the planter, or else they get them from some store designated by him. The commissary or store charges from twenty-five to fifty per cent. interest on the value of the money and supplies advanced or furnished. If any one doubts this statement, let him ask any planter or storekeeper. As a whole, they admit it. They boast that the commissary is the safest and best paying department of the plantation.

A northern white man bought a big farm in Mississippi. Of course, he had a "commissary." When the season was over, he complained that he had made but little money. His southern neighbors asked him questions as to his methods etc. and found that he had charged the cost price for his supplies and had added ten per cent. for profit and had settled with his hands at the actual market value of the cotton at the time it was sold. They said, "Hell, man, you haven't got the right system. You don't make money down here on your cotton except in good years. You make your money off your commissary. Besides, never give your niggers a statement of their accounts. If you do, you will ruin every nigger in the country. Just tell them what they've got coming and pay them off and don't let 'em argue or ask any questions."

That is only part of the "system." The landlord takes the cotton, gins it, sells it at the highest market price, and settles with his tenants at the lowest market price for their "share" of the crop. They play both ends against the middle and get the Negro going and coming. If a Negro objects, he is classed as "an insolent nigger" or a "bad nigger." He is beaten by the "agent" or "boss man" and either driven off the place, or else he admits he is wrong, becomes thoroughly cowed, and then is allowed to remain.

Several years ago, the United States Government started to investigate alleged peonage among Italian laborers in the South. To their surprise and chagrin they ran across very little Italian peonage, but a great deal of Negro peonage. In Phillips County a white lawyer, named Bratton, prosecuted a number of cases for the government and convicted a half-dozen planters.

Recently the price of cotton has, as you know, greatly increased. It was about nine cents a pound in 1904, eleven cents in 1915, twenty cents in 1916, and twenty-eight cents in 1917. The price at present is forty cents. This rise in price has made it difficult to keep the Negroes in debt, and, therefore, they have become restive in their demands for itemized settlements.

That was the situation in 1918. Many Negroes had their cotton taken by the planter in October, 1918, but did not get a settlement until July, 1919. They had never been able to get a statement of their accounts from month to month, hence when July came, how could a man dispute an account made the year before? How could he say that he did not get certain supplies in June 1918, when he did not know until July 1919, what he was charged with?

The Negroes got tired of it. Sixty-eight of them got together and decided to hire a lawyer and get statements of their accounts and a settlement at the right figures. They decided not to hire a Negro lawyer, because they knew that it meant mobbing and death to any Negro lawyer who would have the presumption to take one of these white planters to court. They were afraid to trust any white lawyer in Phillips County for fear their attorney would lay down on them and fail to get results after getting their money. They canvassed the situation and found that the firm of Bratton and

Bratton, white, of Little Rock, was a good, reliable firm, and would fight for a Negro client to the last. They made contracts with this firm to handle all the sixty-eight cases at fifty dollars each in cash and a percentage of the moneys collected from the white planters. Also some of these Negroes and their friends planned to go before the Federal Grand Jury and charge certain white planters with peonage. These men had meetings from time to time for the purpose of collecting the moneys which were to be paid in advance and to place the same in the treasury; also to collect evidence and gather facts which would enable them to successfully prosecute these cases. These meetings had to be secret to prevent harm and danger to the men concerned and to their families.

Meanwhile another organization sprang up. The Negro cotton pickers organized a union to raise the wages of cotton-pickers and refused to pick cotton until they received higher wages for their work. These meetings were secret. Also, at Elaine were a great many Negroes who worked in the saw-mills and who received fair wages, and who refused to allow their wives and daughters to pick cotton or to work for a white man at any price. They did this as a measure of protection to their wives and daughters, who were subject to the advances and insults of white men on the cotton farms. All these movements became known to the white planters and they resolved to break up the whole business and put the Negroes "in their place." It is the unwritten law of the cotton planter that his Negro tenants "must not take the boss man to law." Woe be unto the "insolent nigger" who attempts it. The white men also learned that Negroes were buying guns and plenty of ammunition. The merchants at Helena reported large sales and the express offices also reported shipments of rifles and shell to Negroes. The Negroes had read and heard all about the East St. Louis, Washington, and Chicago riots, and knew of the secret Ku Klux Klan movements among the white people in the South. They knew that race hatred on the part of white people was increasing by leaps and bounds and that riots were liable to break out in that section at any time. They were simply preparing to defend their homes and lives, for experience had taught them that Negroes have no protection at the hands of the law. The police and deputy sheriffs either refuse to check the mobs, or else they join hands with the mobs. The assembling of arms was for purely defensive purposes. No Negro was fool enough to think of an "insurrection" against white people.

While the white men were meeting secretly and discussing means of "nipping the niggers in the bud," matters came to a head very suddenly in an unexpected way. On Sunday, before the riot, John Clem, a white man, from Helena, came to Elaine loaded up and drunk on "white mule." He proceeded to bully and terrorize the whole Negro population of over four hundred people by continuous gun play. The Negroes, to avoid trouble, got off the streets, and phoned to the sheriff at Helena. He failed to act. Monday, Clem was still on a rampage. The Negroes avoided trouble, because they feared that his acts were a part of a plan to start a race riot. Tuesday, some Negroes were holding a meeting in a church at Hoop Spur. A deputy sheriff and a "special agent," white, and a Negro trusty came by in an auto. The white men stopped and proceeded to "investigate" the meeting. They were refused admittance. They attempted to break in and fired into the building. Some Negroes returned the fire, killing the special agent and wounding the deputy sheriff, so it is said. However, when the Negro trusty reported the shooting, he said that they had been fired upon from ambush by two white men and a Negro. The wounded deputy also first reported that the party had been fired upon from ambush by two white men and he was quite sure he saw a Negro running from the scene. Later all mention of the white men was carefully avoided and suppressed, and the entire blame was laid upon the Negroes at the church and it was charged that all of them were armed, that the white men were proceeding peaceably on the road and only got out to fix their car, which just happened to break down right in front of this particular church, and that the Negroes fired on them without any provocation whatever. Later another white man was fired on, and it was claimed that he just happened to be coming along the road an hour later and was shot by Negroes who were at the same church.

It never seemed for a moment unreasonable to the white men to believe that the Negroes would kill and wound white men at the church and then deliberately stay there for an hour or two longer for the purpose of killing another white man. Every sane man knows that those Negroes would have fled from the scene after the first shooting, if they had been guilty.

Anyhow, the hue and cry was raised. "Negro uprising," "Negro insurrection," etc., was sent broadcast. The white planters called their gangs together and a big "nigger hunt" began. They rushed their women and children to Helena by auto and train. Train loads and auto loads of white men, armed to the teeth, came from Marianna and Forrest City, Ark., Memphis, Tenn., and Clarksdale, Miss. Rifles and ammunition were rushed in. The woods were scoured, Negro homes shot into, Negroes who did not know any trouble was brewing were shot and killed on the highways.

Telegrams were sent to Governor Brough. He called for Federal troops and five hundred were rushed from Camp Pike, armed with rifles, cannon, gas masks hand grenades, bombs, and machine- guns. The Colonel took "charge of all strategic points," and "mobilized his men to repel the attack of the black army." The country was scoured for a radius of fifty to one hundred miles, covering all of Phillips and part of adjoining counties, for "Negro insurrectionists."

The soldiers arrested over a thousand Negroes, men and women, and placed them in a "stockade" under heavy guard and kept them there under the most disgusting, unwholesome, and unsanitary conditions. They were not allowed to see friends or attorneys but all of them had to be separately and personally "investigated" by the army officers and a white "committee of seven." Even after "investigation" had proven completely that a Negro was wholly innocent, still no Negro was released until after a white man had appeared and personally "vouched" for him as being a "good nigger." The white man was usually a planter or employer and they refused to "vouch" for the Negroes until the Negroes had given assurance and "guarantees" as to work and wages. Finally, all but two or three hundred were released. All Negroes who owned their own farms or were otherwise independent, were held, as a rule, because no white man would vouch for them. In addition to those held by the soldiers, over three hundred were arrested and placed in the jail at Helena, charged with murder and rioting, and refused bond. They were not allowed to see friends or attorneys and were "investigated" by the "committee of seven." This committee was secret at first. Its membership was not disclosed, but was organized and did its work with the direct sanction of Governor Brough.

The next day, after the first killing of the special agent, which occurred at Hoop Spur, 0. G. Bratton, a son of U. S. Bratton, arrived at Ratio. There he met many Negroes who had employed the firm of Bratton & Bratton to obtain their settlements. The Negroes represented the sixty-eight tenants on the Fairthy plantation. They had had no settlement of their 1918 cotton crop until July 1919, and then no itemized account. Two carloads of their 1919 crop were about to be shipped without settlement and they determined to take the matter into court.

About fifty of them began to pay the cash fees agreed upon. Many had no cash, so they offered him their Liberty Bonds, which he accepted. While collecting this money and giving receipts, a crowd of white men, who were engaged in the "nigger hunt," came upon him. They arrested Bratton and all the Negroes with him and sent them to jail at Helena, where they were imprisoned on charges of "Murder," and held without bond.

Bratton was on the train on his way to Ratio, which is twelve miles from Hoop Spur, and he and the Negro clients had not yet heard of the trouble when they met to close up the payment of the cash fees intended for his firm. All this time the white press of Arkansas kept up a hue and cry to the effect that Bratton was there "inciting an uprising of the Negroes and teaching them social equality." The feeling was so bitter against young Bratton that there were grave threats and fears of his being lynched. The Governor ordered special guards sworn in, patrols were stationed about the jail, and only the utmost precautions prevented the lynching of a man who was not even a lawyer and whose only crime consisted in collecting fees for his father's firm. It is now openly admitted that Bratton is clearly innocent of any part in the trouble, still he was held thirty-one days without bond in jail and then released without trial, because his father was about to obtain justice for Negro tenants.

The saddest and worst feature of the whole miserable slaughter of Negroes was the killing of the four Johnston brothers. They were sons of a prominent and able Negro Presbyterian minister, who is now dead. Their mother is a very prominent woman and was formerly a school teacher. Dr. D. A. E. Johnston was a successful dentist and owned a three-story building in Helena. One brother fought in France and was wounded and gassed in the battle of Chateau-Thierry. Dr. Louis Johnston was a prominent physician and lived in Oklahoma. He had come home on a visit.

On the day of the first trouble the four brothers had gone squirrel hunting early that morning and started for home in the evening, wholly ignorant of the trouble at Hoop Spur. While they were miles out in the woods hunting, word of the trouble reached Helena. A merchant told the deputy sheriffs and posse that he had sold some shells to the Johnstons a day or so before the trouble.

A crowd of men in an auto went to hunt for the Johnstons. They met them returning from the hunt. These white men were supposed friends of the Johnstons. They told them of the trouble and a riot was in progress and that it would be dangerous for any Negro to be on the country roads, especially armed. The Johnstons told them they had just been hunting and had nothing but shot-guns and squirrel shot. They were advised by their friends to turn back and go home by a train that would pass a little station several miles down the road. They took this advice and went to the station to go by rail to Helena. They left their car with a friend, whom they told of the situation. They had bought their tickets and were on the train when up rolled a car with some deputies. They arrested three of the men and took them from the train. The fourth brother, from Oklahoma, also got off. The officers had with them a man named Lilly, a friend of another white man with whom Dentist Johnston had had trouble, the week before. When Dr. Johnston got off the train, the officers told him to go back. He refused, saying, "These men are my brothers. If you arrest them, I will go too." Then the officers said, "Well, if you are one of the Johnston brothers, we want you, too." They then arrested the Oklahoma man, whose only crime was that of being a brother to the other three.

The men were loaded into an auto and the car went back down the same road they had come over. After going a few miles, a crowd of white men appeared, led by the very "white friends" who had warned the Johnstons to take the train. They had telephoned or sent word to the officers as to where they could get the Johnstons. As the mob approached, Lilly and the officers began to get out of the auto. The Johnstons then saw that they had been led into a trap by their supposed "white friends." They were handcuffed, but they tried to put up a fight. Just as Lilly was climbing out of the car, preparing to turn the helpless men over to the mob, Dr. Johnston, although shackled, managed to grab Lilly's pistol from his hand and shot him. The officers and the mob then shot the men literally to pieces. They were sowed with bullets so much so that their faces had to be covered at the funeral, and parts of their bodies were in shreds. The noble mother had to endure the terrible ordeal of seeing four of her fine, promising sons buried in one grave.

The main results of the whole miserable business are as follows: five white men and between twenty-five and fifty Negroes were killed in the riots; the stench of dead bodies could be smelled two miles. One thousand Negroes were arrested and one hundred and twenty-two indicted. Evidence was gathered by a committee consisting of two planters, a cotton factor, a merchant, a banker, the sheriff of the county, and the Mayor of Helena. They are said to have used electric connections on the witness chair to scare the Negroes. Sixty-six men have been tried and convicted-twelve sentenced to death, and fifty-four to penitentiary terms. The trials averaged from five to ten minutes each; no witnesses for the defense were called; no Negroes were on the juries; no change of venue was asked. The work of "cleaning up" our people is not yet finished. The Grand Jury is at work and hundreds are to be indicted on charges of murder, rioting, conspiracy, etc. White lawyers at Helena are preparing to reap a harvest of fat fees from Negroes against whom there is no evidence, but who have saved money and property and Liberty Bonds. The Negroes are to be stripped to the bone.

The Negroes in the Black Belt are much demoralized, discouraged, and depressed. Hundreds are preparing to leave. Many Negro leaders, who have stood by the white people and who have counseled their race to stay here, now have not a word to say and many of them are also preparing to wind up their affairs and get out of the South. Negroes here live in fear and terror, afraid even to discuss the situation except in whispers and to well-known friends.

Governor Brough has issued a statement to the public press that he intends to have *The Defender* and *THE CRISIS* suppressed. The Arkansas Gazette, white, has issued an editorial demanding that Negro leaders give their people "proper advice," and warning them that their race is in danger of annihilation unless Negroes cease to be led by the lure of Liberty and equal political rights and also warning them that the freedom of the Negro from bad economic conditions is not to be obtained by the methods which were resorted to by the Negroes of Phillips County. Also any white man who fights, either in court or elsewhere, for the rights of the Negro is to be put in jail and suffer social and business ostracism from the white people of the South.

OMAHA

For forty years Omaha was ruled by a political, criminal gang that was perhaps the most lawless of any city of its size in the civilized world. There had grown up during that period, a powerful group who lived on the proceeds of organized vice and crime. These included about three hundred and eighty-four (384) houses of prostitution, together with saloons, pool halls, organized bank robbers, organized highway robbers, and professional "con" men and burglars.

"The Crucifixion at Omaha"

THE CRUCIFIXION AT OMAHA

Whenever a plan was made to have a election of officials, certain men in the community would assemble and hold a conference and they would decide what men it would be "safe" to elect, and they would give The Boss for his service a certain sum of money and control of the vice interests, the Police Department, the Police Court, the juries, and then proceed to elect public officials. This condition obtained, without interruption, from the early history of the city until 1908.

Reforms began in 1908 by an early closing law for saloons, followed by laws which took the control of juries and elections from the vice-ring. In 1916 statewide prohibition was carried.

We thus eliminated the whiskey interests which furnished the most of the money for election purposes, the control of the jury and election machinery, from the gang, and the actual disposition of public officers, but we had not eliminated all of the gang. There was still left the Omaha Bee which had been the mouth-piece of the vice-ring, the thugs and murderers who had ruled for years, and these combined to destroy the present city administration and regain control of the Police Department, which was absolutely necessary for the continuation of the reign and control of vice.

In order to accomplish this, the Omaha Bee, assisted at times by the other daily papers, began a campaign of slander and vituperation against the Police Department of the City of Omaha, and in order to make it effective they chose a line of propaganda to the effect that Negro men were attacking white women, assaulting them with intent to commit rape, and actually committing rape, with the connivance of the Police Department. They made a majority of the people in Omaha believe that all Negro men were disposed to commit the crime of rape on white women.

For years there has been much illegal cohabitation of whites and blacks in Omaha, with about fifteen assignation houses where colored men met white prostitutes. Leading colored citizens asked the police to suppress these dens, but when this was begun, it only increased the slander and vituperation of the Omaha Bee, the organ of the vice-ring. This was kept up successfully until the people believed that the police were invading private property without warrant of law and arresting law-abiding citizens.

There was still left in the Police Department from the old regime a large percentage of the police officers protected by Civil Service, who were loyal to the old vice-ring, and they were doing everything within their power to hamper and discredit the honest efforts of the present city administration to enforce the law. The result of this was that together with the campaign of the newspapers, the morale of the Police Department was broken down and the city administration was unable, in the brief space of time that it had been in office, to get rid of these discordant elements. There was, furthermore, in connection with these men, fathered by these same influences, an organized gang determined to wreck the administration at any cost, and they deliberately organized a mob; they furnished it with money and liquor, and the leaders of the old vice-ring stood around in the mob, urging the men to go in and assist in wrecking the Court House, lynch the Negro, and kill the Mayor of the City and other officials.

Both Brown, who was lynched, and the woman who accused him belonged to the under-world which met at the houses of assignation. They had quarreled and the woman "got back" at Brown by alleging attempted assault. It is said that at the time she was wearing a diamond ring given her by Brown.

A Southern Colored Woman

A letter was written to the editor of *The Crisis* by a Southern Black Women who had grown tired of the violence against Black people being unanswered by the Black men in the community. She delighted in the fact that Black men in Washington and Chicago fought back.

The Washington riot gave me the thrill that comes once in a lifetime. I was alone when I read between the lines of the morning paper that at last our men had stood like men, struck back, were no longer dumb, driven cattle. When I could no longer read for my streaming tears, I stood up, alone in my room, held both hands high over my head and exclaimed aloud: "Oh, I thank God, thank God!" When I remember anything after this, I was prone on my bed, beating the pillow with both fists, laughing and crying, whimpering like a whipped child, for sheer gladness and madness. The pent-up humiliation, grief and horror of a life time—half a century—was being stripped from me. Only colored women of the south know the extreme in suffering and humiliation.

We know how many insults we have borne silently, for we have hidden many of them from our men because we did not want them to die needlessly in our defense; we know the sorrow of seeing our boys and girls grow up, the swift stab of the heart at night to the sound of a strange foot-step, the feel of a tigress to spring and claw the white man with his lustful look at our comely daughters, the deep humiliation of sitting in the Jim Crow part of a street car and hear the white man laugh and discuss us, point out the good and bad points of our bodies. God alone knows the many things colored women have borne here in the South in silence.

And, too, a woman loves a strong man, she delights to feel that her man can protect her, fight for her, if necessary, save her.

No woman loves a weakling, a coward, be she white or black, and some of us have been near to thinking our men cowards, but thank God for Washington colored men! All honor to them, for they first blazed the way and right swiftly did Chicago men follow. They put new hope, a new vision in their almost despairing women. God grant that our men everywhere refrain from strife, provoke no quarrel, but that they protect their women and homes at any cost.

A Southern Colored Woman
I'm sure the editor will understand why I cannot sign my name.

Blacks who fought back and those who didn't were punished severely for their 'role' in the riots. In some cases, their role was nothing more than running from the mob. For example, according to the *Chicago Tribune* 16-year-old Walter Colvin and 17-year-old Charles Johnson were sentenced to life in prison. Moreover, several men in the Elaine, Arkansas riot were arrested, tried, and sentenced to life in prison. However, after years in jail, with help from leaders including Ida B. Wells-Barnett, the final six of the Black men who had been held were released in 1923 according to the November 17th *Pittsburg Courier*.

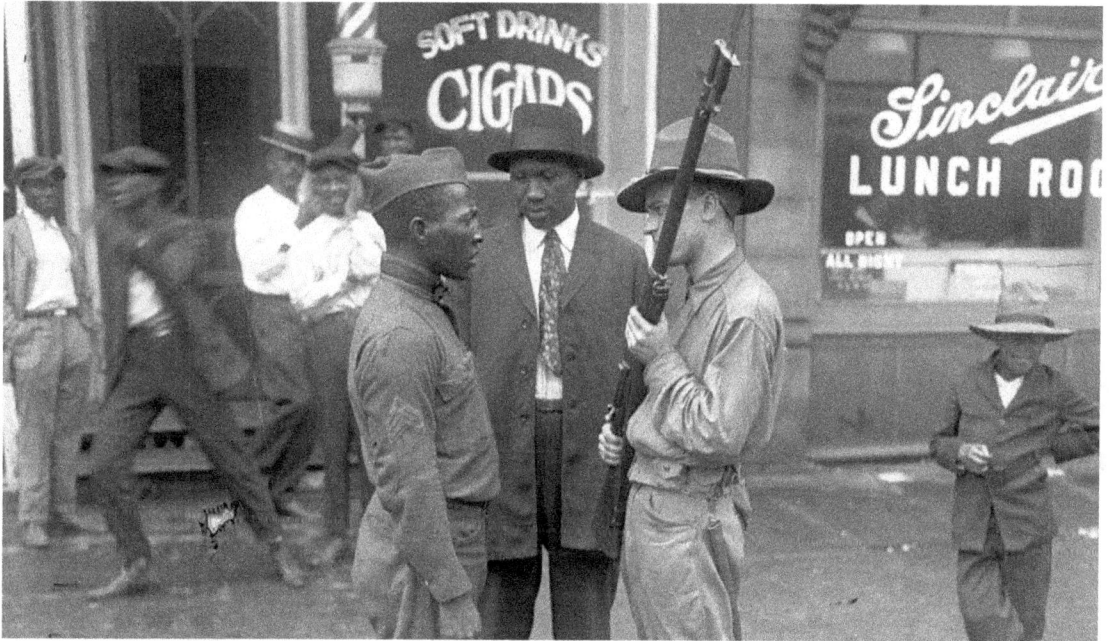

ABOUT THE AUTHOR

Tiffany Lee is the coauthor of the work, *Legendary East St. Louisans: An African American Series,* a book that covers the bios of African-American influencers over a one-hundred-year period. She also compiled several anthologies covering former slaves lives into the series *Steal Away: Freed Slaves Stories of Life on the Plantation.* In her works, she covers marginalized voices and believes in giving voice to the voiceless. In her work commemorating the 1917 East St. Louis Race Riots, she became overwhelmed by the victim's stories that had rarely been heard; and thus, began research to assure that victims of riots stories were told. She is a lecturer at Harris Stowe State University and Saint Louis Community College.

APPENDIX

Article published *joking* about Boston Race Riots.

BOBALITION 1816

Dreadful Riot on Negro Hill!

O Read wid datention de Melancholly Tale and he send you yelling to your bed!

Copy of an intercepted letter from PHILLIS, to her Sister in the country, describing the Riot on Negro Hill.

JOHN MERCER LANGSTON

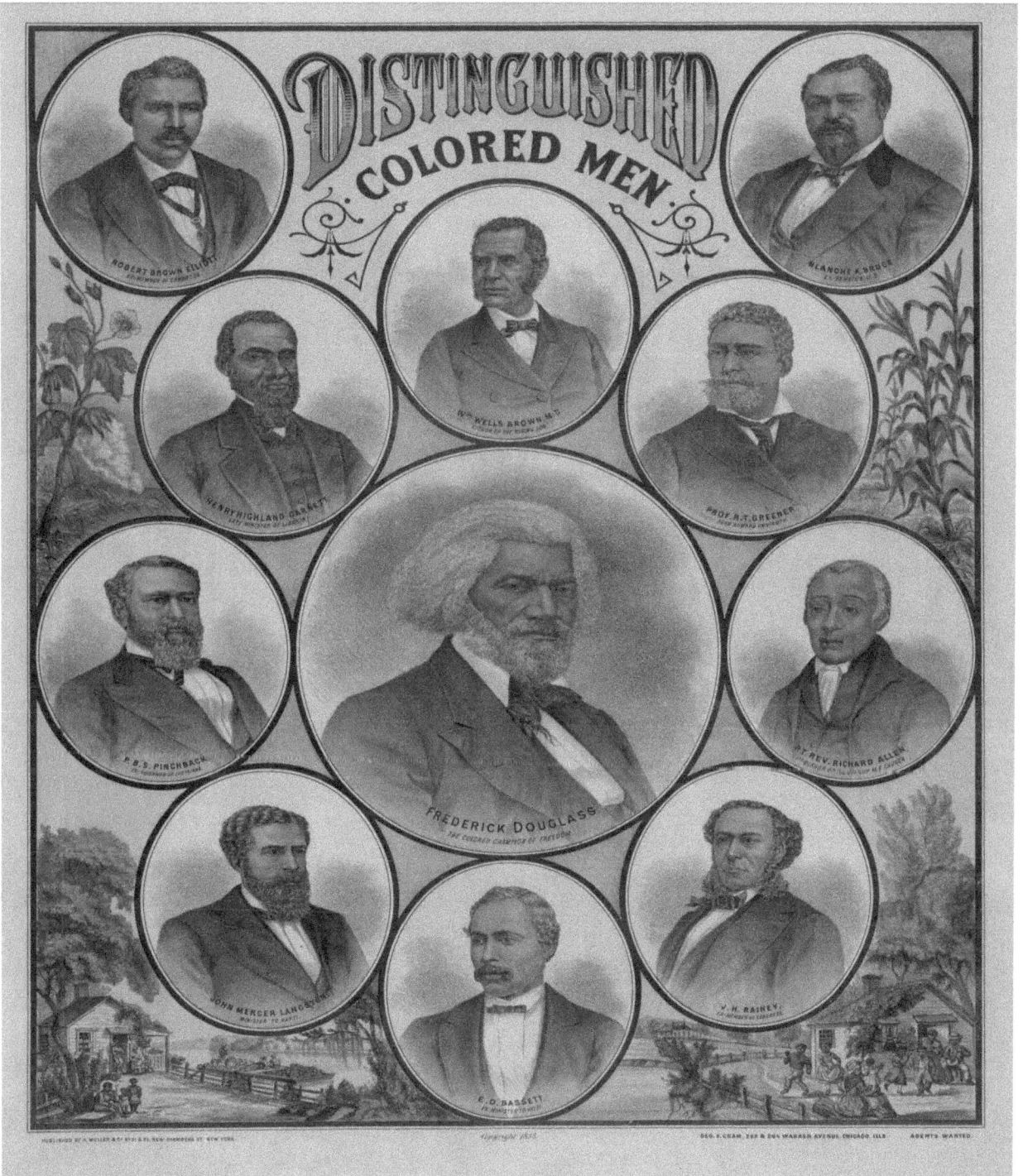

JOHN MERCER LANGSTON AND OTHER PROMINENT BLACK CITIZENS.

SOURCES

[1] During my research, I believed that I noted a race riot in the late 1700's in New York, but I have been unable to find that article.

[2] http://www.ric.edu/northburialground/tours_1824-riot.html

[3] *Sundown Towns: A Hidden Dimension of American Racism*

[4] *Encyclopedia of Race Riots.*

[5] *Rioting in America, pg 89*

[6] *Race and the City: Work, Community, and Protest in Cincinnati, 1820-1970*

[7] *The Weekly Perrysburg Journal*, March 18th 1963

[8] Friday, March 27, 1863. Page 10.

[9] *The Encyclopedia of Race Riots*

[10] Art and Picture Collection, The New York Public Library. "New York -- Hanging And Burning A Negro In Clarkson Street." New York Public Library Digital Collections. Accessed August 6, 2019. http://digitalcollections.nypl.org/items/510d47e1-281d-a3d9-e040-e00a18064a99

[11] Art and Picture Collection, The New York Public Library. "New York -- Burning of the Second Avenue armory." The New York Public Library Digital Collections. 188?. http://digitalcollections.nypl.org/items/510d47e1-2816-a3d9-e040-e00a18064a99

[12] Nast, Thomas, Artist. "This is a white man's government" "We regard the Reconstruction Acts so called of Congress as usurpations, and unconstitutional, revolutionary, and void" - Democratic Platform / / Th. Nast. United States, 1868. Photograph. https://www.loc.gov/item/98513794/.

[13] For more on the White League, see https://digitallibrary.tulane.edu/islandora/object/tulane%3A13208

[14] Waud, Alfred R. , Artist. Scenes in Memphis, Tennessee, during the riot. Memphis Tennessee, 1866. Photograph. https://www.loc.gov/item/94507780/.

[15] The Freedmen's Bureau Online, Records of the Assistant Commissioner for the State of Tennessee Bureau of Refugees, Freedmen, and Abandoned Lands, 1865-1869
National Archives Microfilm Publication M999, roll 34
"Reports of Outrages, Riots and Murders, Jan. 15, 1866 - Aug. 12, 1868"

[16] https://play.google.com/books/reader?id=ep8FAAAAQAAJ&hl=en&pg=GBS.PA31

[17] *The Journal of Negro History.* "The Memphis Riots of 1866."

[18] http://freedmensbureau.com/tennessee/outrages/memphisriot.htm

[19] Nast, Thomas, Artist. *The massacre at New Orleans*. Louisiana New Orleans, 1867. Photograph. https://www.loc.gov/item/2009617747/.

[20] https://cdn.loc.gov/service/rbc/rbaapc/20600/20600.pdf

[21] http://hd.housedivided.dickinson.edu/node/45565

[22] The Clarion-Ledger · Thu, Jul 13, 1871 · Page 2

[23] Knopf, Terry. Journal of Black Studies. Vol. 4. No. 3 Mar., 1974 "Race, Riots and Reporting." Pg 307.

[24] https://www.newspapers.com/image/167961323

[25] Dorothy Sterling, ed., The Trouble They Seen: The Story of Reconstruction in the Words of African Americans (Da capo Press, 1994), 442–443.

[26] Philadelphia Inquirer, September 9th 1875.

[27] Encyclopedia of Race Riots, page 604.

[28] https://dnr.mo.gov/shpo/nps-nr/98001108.pdf

[29] Newspaper.com/image/350275340, Chicago Tribune, Mon, April 20, 1903

[30] https://digital.lib.niu.edu/islandora/object/niu-gildedage%3A24051

[31] *Crisis* Newspaper Article: "The Massacre of East St. Louis", page 228.

[32] *St. Louis Post Dispatch.*"Alibi Offered at Negro Dentist's Trial for Murder." Mar. 26, 1919.

[33] *Chicago Tribune*. "High Spots in the Omaha Race Riot." Sept.29, 1919.

[34] *Sundown Towns: A Hidden Dimension of American Racism*

[35] https://www.ccpl.org/charleston-time-machine/charleston-riot-1919#_edn3

[36] *The Crisis*. "The Real Cause of Race Riots." December, 1919.